101 Great Gifts Kids Can Make

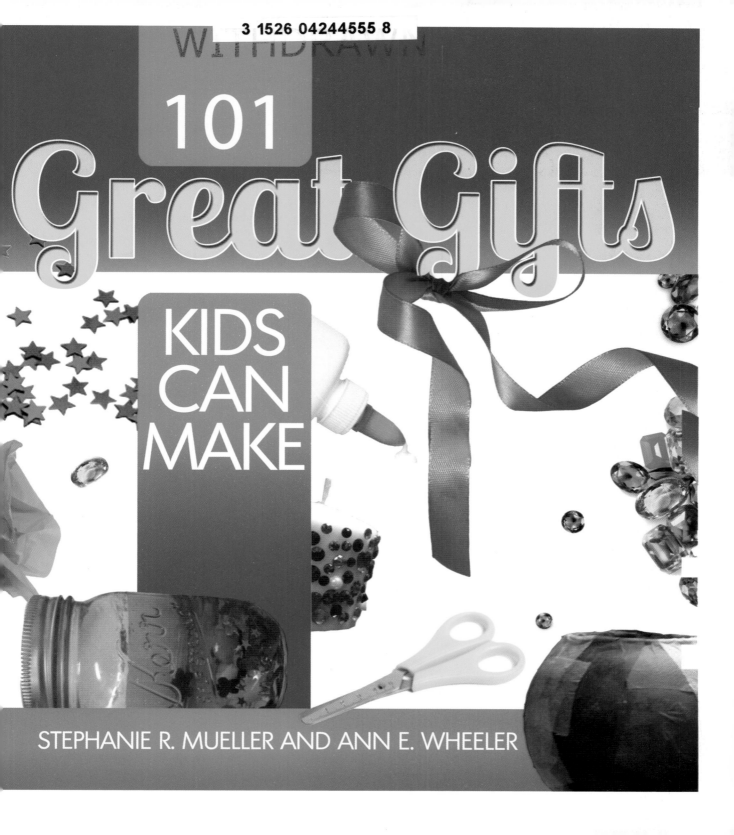

101
Great Gifts

KIDS CAN MAKE

STEPHANIE R. MUELLER AND ANN E. WHEELER

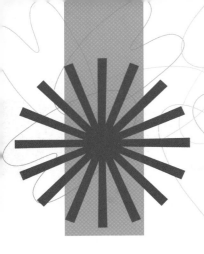

Bulk purchase

Gryphon House books are available for special premiums and sales promotions as well as for fund-raising use. Special editions or book excerpts also can be created to specification. For details, contact the Director of Marketing at Gryphon House.

Disclaimer

Gryphon House, Inc. and the authors cannot be held responsible for damage, mishap, or injury incurred during the use of or because of activities in this book. Appropriate and reasonable caution and adult supervision of children involved in activities and corresponding to the age and capability of each child involved is recommended at all times. Do not leave children unattended at any time. Observe safety and caution at all times.

Dedication

From Stephanie

Thank you to my parents and to my fellow educators, who inspired and encouraged my creative side.
To my husband, Michael, who is so patient and supportive.
To my daughters, Elsa and Greta, the two greatest gifts this mom could have.

From Ann

To Tony and Nick, thank you for your love and support.
To Ellie Newby (otherwise known as Mom) and Regina Rice, thank you for your dedication to the field of early child care and education. I am so grateful to have had such wonderful mentors.

101 Great Gifts Kids Can Make
Stephanie Mueller and Ann Wheeler
Illustrations: Mary Rojas
(c) 2012 Stephanie Mueller and Ann Wheeler

Published by Gryphon House, Inc.
PO Box 10, Lewisville, NC 27023
800.638.0928; 877.638.7576 (fax)

Visit us on the web at www.gryphonhouse.com

Cover Art: Projects created by McKenzie and her dad, Stuart.

Library of Congress Cataloging-in-Publication Information:

Mueller, Stephanie R.
    101 great gifts kids can make / Stephanie Mueller and Ann Wheeler.
    p.cm.
Includes index.
ISBN 978-0-87659-414-8
1. Handicraft. 2. Gifts. 3. Creative activities and seat work. I.
Wheeler, Ann E. II. Title. III. Title: One hundred and one great gifts
kids can make. IV. Title: One hundred one great gifts kids can make.
TT157.M7742 2012
745.5--dc23
                                2011049683

Table of Contents

Introduction 7

Chapter 1—Fun with Photos!

Easiest-Ever Photo Frame 12
Craft Stick Picture Frame................................13
Fun Frame..14
Classy Photo Frame 15
Framing with Foam..16
Cup Photo Holder...17
Tabletop Photo Holder.....................................18
Monitor Photo Holder 20
"My Year" Photo Album...................................22
Accordion Photo Album....................................24
Photo Collage Box...26

Chapter 2—A Garden of Gifts

A Beautiful Bow-quet.......................................28
"Sweet Treat" Flowers 29
"Say Cheese" Flowers.......................................30
Portable Vase...31
A Sticky Flower Arrangement.......................32
Garden Marker 33
Love Bug Plant Stake 34
Mini Birdbath...35
Watering Can..36
Terra-Cotta Music Makers 38
Wind Catcher..40

Chapter 3—Come Play with Me

Picture Puzzle...42
I Spy Fun...43
Play-with-Me Game Box....................................44

Take-Along Art Box...46
Coupon Pocket..47
Activity Calendar 48
Family Story Notebook.....................................50
"Come Cook with Me" Jar................................52
Oatmeal Bar Cookies 54
Pack a Snack...56

Chapter 4—Office Originals

Weaving Band Pencil Holder 58
Craft Foam Pencil Critter 59
Mosaic-Bottle Organizers 60
Made-It-Myself Mouse Pad...............................61
Sticky Note Magnet...62
Clip-to-It Board 64
Creative Calendar..66
Corky Note Board 67
Layer Jar Paperweight 68
Jiffy Juice-Lid Magnet 69
Mat Board Magnet 70
Recycled Magnet 72
Family Foam Magnets 73
Stress Ball Sock..74

Chapter 5—Household Helps

Personalized Coasters 76
Beautiful Basket Liner 77
Chip Clip..78
Candy Dish..80
Octopus Duster 82
Collage Bookmark..83
Craft Stick Bookmark..84

"Look What I Made!" Magnet 85
Write-and-Wipe Board.............................86
French Memo Board 88
Button-Up Bulletin Board 90
Treasure Box...91
All Smiles Key Chain 92
Car Visor Clip 94

Chapter 6—Decorations to Display

Nature Plaque..96
Decorative Tile 97
"Sun-sational" Sun Catcher 98
See-Through Ornament...............................100
Seasonal Switch Plate Cover 101
Fragrant Door Hanger 102
Decorative Door Hanger 104
Pictures on My Window..............................105
Colorful Wall Hanging...............................106
"Happy Holidays" Wreath............................108
Table Wreath 110
Etched Candle 111
Beaded Candle 112
Colorful Candle 113
Stained Glass Candleholder 114
Beaded Ornament...................................115
Cinnamon Family 116
Jazzy Jigsaw Pin 118

Chapter 7—Say It with a Card

A "Hand-y" Card.....................................120
Painted Postcards....................................121
Foil Etched Card 122
Lacing Card 124
Polka-Dot Frame Card 126
Old Clothes Patch Card 127
Peekaboo Card.......................................128
Handprint Blossoms..................................130
Lift-the-Flap Card 131

Stamped Stationery 132
Swirl Card 133
Woven Card 134

Chapter 8—Wrap It Up!

Bubble-Wrap Paper...................................138
Bubble Blowing Wrapping Paper 139
Salty Wrapping Paper Sensation 140
Wrapping Paper Bonanza 141
Tape Print Gift Bag 142
"My Feet" Gift Bag 144
Sponging Gift Bag....................................146
"Wrap It Up" Canister 147
Decorative Gift Box..................................148
Papier-Mâché Gift Box...............................149
Fancy Gift Basket 150
Paper-Plate Basket 152

List of Common and Uncommon
    Holidays..153
Materials List..157

Index

Index..159

Introduction

When young children make something unique to give as a special gift for a loved one, they feel proud and successful about what they can do and share. Often these child-made gifts are treasured for years to come. With the appropriate materials, the freedom to be creative, and a little guidance, the possibilities for child-made gifts are infinite.

101 Great Gifts Kids Can Make is full of gift-making activities for children three to eight years old. The ideas can be used with a group of children or with one child. Most of the ideas use easy-to-find materials, and many ideas cost only a few cents to make.

What Is a Great Gift?

- It is unique to the child—created without adult-imposed patterns or standards, so no two are alike.
- It is open to imagination and creativity—the child's ideas, choices, and personality are integrated.
- It is "owned" by the child—the child made it, investing thought, time, and energy; therefore, the gift means more when given to someone else.
- It is made with minimal adult help—the adult selects and sets up appropriate materials for each activity, then steps back as the child creates.

How to Use This Book

Table of Contents

The chapters are divided by characteristics unique to the materials or type of gift. This makes the gift ideas appropriate for a wide variety of holidays and special occasions.

Activities

Materials

Most materials are readily available or easily obtained. Whenever possible, we suggest alternative ideas to offer flexibility based on the materials that may be on hand. Unless otherwise noted, the term *paint* indicates tempera paint, and *glue* specifies white glue. Always use materials that are appropriate for young children, such as nontoxic paints and

markers and child-size scissors. A list of commonly used Great Gift materials is on page 157.

Before Beginning

Some activities include a "Before Beginning" icon, which indicates that some adult preparation is required before the child gets involved in the activity.

Make Your Great Gift

While adults can use the directions included in each activity to guide the gift-making process, the projects are the child's to create. We believe the process, the creative freedom, and the value of giving are more important than the physical appearance of the end product.

As with any activity, consider the developmental level and abilities of each individual child. All gift-making materials should be child-safe and nontoxic. These activities are designed for children ages three and up; some children will need help. We recommend close adult supervision at all times as your child creates Great Gifts.

To prepare for all activities, cover the workspace, provide a smock to cover the child's clothing, and select a safe place for wet projects to dry. Also, have an appropriate writing utensil handy to write the date and the child's name on the gift.

Variation

Several activities can be modified to create a whole new gift-giving project.

Helpful Hints

Many activities include ideas to help children complete the projects, including time- and money-saving tips, options for materials, and alternative steps.

Seasonal Suggestions

Some activities include suggestions to make them unique to certain holidays or special occasions. By simply changing the color of paint or type of paper used, a child-made gift can become uniquely seasonal. We also encourage readers to come up with adaptations to fit their specific needs.

Index

Use the index to find gifts to make based on the materials you have at hand or a holiday or occasion you want to celebrate.

Why We Wrote This Book

We noticed a need for this book when we tried to locate gift-making ideas appropriate for young children. In addition, the attendance at workshops we presented on this subject has been large, and the children who have made gifts have been enthusiastic.

We have used ideas in this book as early childhood teachers and as parents. Some are new ideas using modern materials; others are traditional gifts or familiar art activities that have been modified to fit the developmental levels of young children.

Our goal is for all involved to experience the joy that can be found in giving and receiving unique child-made gifts.

Fun with Photos!

Make frames, albums, and other personal gifts using children's photographs.

Easiest-Ever Photo Frame

Trim contact paper to frame a favorite photo.

Materials

clear contact paper

card stock or lightweight cardboard

glue stick

photo of child

tissue paper scraps, colored cellophane, stickers

magnetic tape

Before Beginning

Cut the card stock to the desired size and shape. It should be larger than the photograph with plenty of room for the photo and a border of collage material.

Make Your Great Gift

1. Glue the photo to the center of the card stock.
2. Arrange and glue flat collage materials, such as tissue paper scraps, colored cellophane pieces, and stickers, on the surface of the card stock around the photo.
3. Cover both sides with clear contact paper, and firmly press it down on the photo and collage materials.
4. Trim the contact paper to the edges of the card stock. Press to seal.
5. Place a piece of magnetic tape on the back of the frame.

Seasonal Suggestion

■ The card stock can be cut into a holiday shape, such as a heart for Valentine's Day or a flower for Mother's Day. Heart-shaped stickers can be one of the collage materials. For autumn, cut the card stock into a leaf shape, and add leaf-shaped foil confetti.

Craft Stick Picture Frame

Collage materials and glue turn these plain sticks into a fabulous frame.

Make Your Great Gift

1. Arrange four craft sticks into a square. The ends of the craft sticks need to overlap at the corners. Glue the corners together.
2. Glue collage materials such as aquarium gravel, buttons, and plastic gemstones to the craft stick frame.
3. After the glue dries, place a strip of magnetic tape on the back of each corner of the frame.

Helpful Hints

■ Glue the craft stick frame together, and allow it to dry before decorating with collage materials.

■ Adapt this gift to fit a special occasion by drawing a picture and dictating a message to the intended recipient. Secure the picture and message in the frame with clear tape.

Materials

craft sticks

glue

aquarium gravel, small pebbles, plastic buttons, or plastic gemstones

magnetic tape

Fun Frame

Turn cardboard into a wonderfully festive frame.

Materials

cardboard, cut to frame a 5" x 7" piece of paper

lightweight collage materials, such as paper scraps, ribbon, and foil

glue

paper, 5" x 7"

crayons or markers

magnetic tape

tape

Make Your Great Gift

1. Decorate the cardboard frame with the lightweight collage materials.
2. While the glue dries, use markers or crayons to draw a picture for the recipient of the frame on the 5" x 7" paper.
3. Place a strip of magnetic tape along the back of the top of the frame.
4. Put the artwork in the frame, and secure it to the back of the frame with tape.

Helpful Hints

- To create straight, even frames, use mat board that frames a 5" x 7" picture as a pattern to trace the frame shape onto the cardboard rectangle.
- Use thin cardboard that is easily cut with scissors.

Classy Photo Frame

Enhance clear Plexiglas frames by adding buttons, sequins, and other collage materials.

Before Beginning

Cut a piece of scrap paper the approximate size and shape of the photo. Tape onto center of Plexiglas frame.

Make Your Great Gift

1. Glue buttons and sequins on the Plexiglas that is not covered by the paper.
2. After the glue dries, remove the scrap paper center, and insert the photo in the frame.

Helpful Hints

- Use colored, nontoxic permanent markers instead of collage materials to create a see-through picture or to write a simple message.
- Use glitter glue to add sparkle to the collage material border.

Seasonal Suggestion

- Use collage materials that relate to the season or occasion. For example, add school-theme stickers for a teacher gift, or add blue and silver beads for Hanukkah.

Materials

Plexiglas frames, with or without magnets

glue, clear drying

scrap paper

colorful buttons

sequins

tape

Framing with Foam

Construct and decorate a photo frame using colored foam, collage materials, and magnetic tape.

Materials

colored craft foam, two colors

scissors

glue

lightweight collage material, such as beads, sequins, small foam pieces, or small buttons

magnetic tape strip, cut into pieces

photo, small

Before Beginning

Trace a shape onto craft foam or create your own shape. Cut a pair of shapes for each frame, one piece from each color of foam. Cut a smaller shape out of the middle of one of the pieces. This becomes the top of the frame.

Make Your Great Gift

1. Glue collage materials on the outer frame piece.
2. Glue the outer frame piece to the back counterpart. Leave a slit between the two pieces at the top to slide in the photo or picture.
3. After the frame is dry, put a strip of magnetic tape on the back of the frame.
4. Use the cut-out center portion piece as a pattern for trimming the photo before it is inserted into the frame.

Helpful Hints

■ Thin craft foam works best. Foam shelf liner could be substituted.
■ Trace the child's hand for a personal touch, and cut out the center of her palm for the photo.

Seasonal Suggestion

■ Use simple people shapes with a circle cut out for the photo. Decorate with wallpaper scraps, cloth scraps, ribbon, and yarn. Wonderful for Grandparents' Day, Mother's Day, and Father's Day!

Cup Photo Holder

A cup and a cardboard tube become a fancy picture display.

Before Beginning

Turn the cup upside down, and cut a hole in the bottom large enough for the cardboard tube to slide inside. Approximately 1"-2" of the cardboard tube should be left at the bottom of the cup. Cut 1" slits on opposite sides of the protruding end of the tube.

Make Your Great Gift

1. Cover the cup and tube with paint, using the sponge paintbrush.
2. After the paint dries, decorate the painted cup and tube using glue and plastic beads or jewels.
3. Slide the photo into the slits at the top end of the tube. The tube should hold the picture in place; most of the picture will be visible above the holder.

Seasonal Suggestion

■ Create a festive holiday photo holder by using foil shapes or gold and silver colored buttons in place of the plastic jewels. Or, use metallic colors of paint.

Materials

solid-color paper party cup, 8 or 9 oz.

cardboard wrapping paper tube, cut into a 6" section

paint

sponge paintbrush

glue

plastic beads or jewels

photo of child

Tabletop Photo Holder

Display a precious photo in a holder made from self-hardening clay.

Materials

self-hardening clay, plain or colored

metal spatula

photo of child

thin paintbrush

tempera paint

Make Your Great Gift

1. Work a small, ball-sized piece of clay into a solid, freestanding shape.
2. If desired, use multiple colors of clay to add designs and features to the creation. Leave a space on the top for a slit for the photo.
3. Using the metal spatula, cut a slit in the top of the holder approximately 1"-2" in length. Cut the slit deep and long enough so that it will hold a photo upright.
4. After the clay dries, paint the clay holder using a paintbrush and tempera paint.
5. Allow the paint to dry. Slide the photo into the slit to complete this personal gift.

Helpful Hints

- Cover the photo with laminate or clear contact paper for added durability.
- Using a toothpick, etch your name on the bottom of the photo holder before it dries.

Seasonal Suggestions

- Create a chunky heart-shaped photo holder for Valentine's Day by forming a thick circle shape, making a dent on one edge, and pinching the clay to a point on the other to produce a heart.
- Experiment with making assorted types of ball shapes for Father's Day. For example, create a golf ball by rolling white clay into a ball and making indentations with an unsharpened pencil.

Monitor Photo Holder

Create a photo holder for a computer monitor using juice-can lids and craft foam.

Materials

2 metal juice-can lids

tape

self-adhesive craft foam

scrap paper

glue

collage materials, such as craft foam pieces, buttons, or sequins

photo

Before Beginning

Fold two juice lids at a 90-degree angle over the edge of a counter or other sturdy object.

Make Your Great Gift

1. Hold the two juice lids so that two flat surfaces of the lids are back-to-back, forming a handle, which will sit on the monitor. The circle forms the front of the photo holder. Tape these two pieces together temporarily.
2. Trace this circle onto the craft foam, and cut it out.
3. Pull off the paper backing from the craft foam, and adhere it to the circle portion of the taped lids. The tape can be removed at this point, because the foam's adhesive backing should hold the juice lids in place.
4. Cut out a paper circle, smaller than the foam circle, and tape it in the center of the foam.
5. Glue collage materials around the border space remaining on the foam. Allow glue to dry.
6. If desired, place collage pieces on the remaining sticky foam back so that they stick out from behind.
7. Remove the paper circle, and replace it with the photo cut in the same circle shape. Tape or glue into place.
8. Place the photo holder so that the "handle" portion sits on the top of a computer monitor.

Helpful Hints

- Save on the cost of materials by using poster board cut into a circle instead of craft foam. Glue it to the metal circle surface.
- If the holder does not stay on the monitor, bend the "handle" portion downward a bit.
- Use regular craft foam, and glue it to the metal circle surface.
- Add yarn hair, pipe cleaner arms and legs, or other items to turn this into a "person" or a creature related to a specific occasion, such as a pumpkin for Halloween.

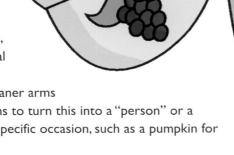

Seasonal Suggestion

- Cut foam into another shape, such as a heart, and use appropriate decorations, for a Valentine's Day gift. Adapt for any holiday or occasion.

"My Year" Photo Album

Display favorite memories in this photo album made of sandwich bags.

Materials

5 zipper-seal plastic sandwich bags

2 thin cardboard squares, cut to the size of the sandwich bags

photos of the child throughout the year

hole punch

yarn

glue

collage materials

Make Your Great Gift

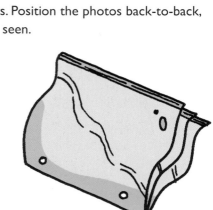

1. Decorate one side of each cardboard square using glue and collage materials.
2. While the glue is drying, look through photos from throughout the year. Choose 10 to use.
3. Using the hole punch, make two holes along one side of each cardboard square. Make sure that the two holes are about 4" apart. Then place holes in the same location along one side of each sandwich bag, making sure that the zipper seal is at the top.
4. Place the photos inside the five sandwich bags. Position the photos back-to-back, two to a bag, so that all of the photos can be seen.
5. Thread yarn through holes in the sandwich bags to bind them together, adding a decorated square to create a front and back cover. Tie the yarn in a bow to hold all of the photo album pages firmly in place.
6. Write your name and the date on the inside front cover of the album.
7. Tie a wide ribbon around the album to add to the gift's appearance and help keep everything together.

Seasonal Suggestions

- Create a winter holiday gift with collage materials such as shredded Mylar, seasonal confetti, wrapping paper scraps, and ribbon.
- Use a photo that features a fun holiday prop, such as reindeer antlers, a flag, or Easter bunny ears. Trim the photo, then glue to the front of the album.

Accordion Photo Album

Index cards are an inexpensive way to create a fun photo display.

Materials

6 photos of child

8 unruled 4" x 6" index cards

colored pencils

glue

clear packing tape

black marker

ribbon

Make Your Great Gift

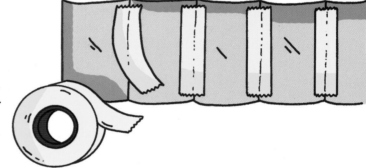

1. Choose six photos for the photo album.
2. Use colored pencils to decorate two index cards.
3. Glue each photo to an undecorated index card.
4. Lay the eight index cards on a table with the pictures and pencil drawings facedown. Place the cards so that the longer sides are touching end to end. Make sure that one decorated card is on each end of the row and the photo cards are in the middle.
5. Use clear packing tape to secure all of the ends together on the backs of the cards. Then turn the row of index cards over, and secure the front ends with tape. Fold the cards back and forth, accordion style, with the pencil drawings showing outward on the front and back cards.
6. Write a short message or greeting to the recipient of the photo album inside the front card.
7. Tie a ribbon around the photo album.

Helpful Hints

- To protect the photo album, laminate or cover it with clear contact paper. Do not use heavy laminating because the cards will not fold.
- Write why the photo is important to you on the back of the corresponding index card.

Seasonal Suggestion

■ Turn this photo display into a great winter holiday gift. Take pictures during each major holiday throughout the calendar year. Place all of these photos on the index cards in chronological order. Then, take a current photo of a traditional winter holiday activity. Use this photo as the last card in the album. Use metallic crayons to decorate the front cover card, and wrap the album in metallic ribbon.

Photo Collage Box

Treasures will have a special place in this box created using a child's photo.

Materials

photo(s) of child

copy machine

scissors

small cardboard box

watered-down glue

paintbrush

Before Beginning

Select one or several photos. Make several copies of the photo on a copy machine. These can be color or black-and-white copies.

Make Your Great Gift

1. Cut out the copies of the photo.
2. Use watered-down glue and a thin paintbrush to glue the pictures on the box lid. Arrange the pictures so that they overlap.
3. While the lid dries, dictate a note to the recipient of the gift. Write it on a notecard, and place it inside the bottom half of the box. Decorate the box bottom, too.

Helpful Hints

- The cardboard box used for this project must be thick and sturdy. Cardboard jewelry boxes, checkbook boxes, and small shoeboxes all work well.
- Paint a thin coat of watered-down glue over the completed box to adhere any loose picture edges.
- Many copy machines have a photo setting that will improve the appearance of copied photographs.
- If you do not have a copy machine available, consider covering the box with pictures drawn just for this project.

A Garden of Gifts

Keep springtime alive with child-made flowers and outdoor decorations.

A Beautiful Bow-quet

Make a beautiful bouquet of flowers using colorful stick-on bows.

Materials

stick-on bows, new or used

green poster board or card stock, cut into 12" x 1" strips

sheets of colored tissue paper

small stickers

ribbon

Make Your Great Gift

1. Choose several colors of bows.
2. Stick one bow near the top of each strip of green poster board or card stock to create flowers with stems. Used bows may have lost some of their stickiness and will need to be glued in place.
3. Decorate a sheet of tissue paper with small stickers.
4. Wrap the bow "flowers" in the decorated tissue paper, and tie a ribbon around the tissue to secure the bouquet.

Helpful Hints

■ Peel the paper backing off of the stick-on bows.
■ Buy tissue paper and bows during post-holiday sales.

Seasonal Suggestion

■ Use seasonal stickers to make this gift holiday specific. For example, shamrock stickers could be used for a St. Patrick's Day bouquet. Red bows on green stems, with red and green tissue paper, would make a beautiful Christmas gift.

Glue

"Sweet Treat" Flowers

Make someone's taste buds smile with these yummy flowers.

Make Your Great Gift

1. Decorate several cupcake liners and a 5" x 4½" piece of green card stock with markers.
2. Wrap each piece of candy in foil or cellophane cut into a square.
3. Place several drops of glue in the center of each cupcake liner, then place a wrapped candy in the middle of each liner.
4. When the glue is dry, create the flower stems by taping a doubled green pipe cleaner to the back of each cupcake liner. Twist the ends of the pipe cleaner together to create a short, thick stem.
5. Help the child roll the card stock into a cone, decorated side out, and secure it with tape. Place the flowers inside the cone.

Variation

■ Instead of candy, glue lightweight, colorful collage materials, such as tissue paper scraps, to fill the cupcake liners.

Helpful Hint

■ Purchasing individually wrapped candy will discourage tasting the creations.

Seasonal Suggestion

■ Cupcake liners with festive patterns are available at local craft stores, party-supply stores, and supermarkets.

Materials

cupcake liners
green card stock, cut into 5" x 4½" pieces
markers
individually wrapped hard candy
foil or colored cellophane, cut into 3" squares
glue
clear tape
green pipe cleaners, folded in half

CHAPTER 2 A Garden of Gifts

"Say Cheese" Flowers

Make someone smile with these card stock flowers featuring the child's photos.

Materials

various colors of card stock or recycled cardboard scraps (e.g., cereal or cracker boxes), cut into flower shapes

crayons or markers

small photo of child

green pipe cleaners

clear tape

glue

card stock, 1 full sheet

Before Beginning

Cut card stock into 4" x 4" flower shapes.

Make Your Great Gift

1. Decorate at least three or four flower shapes with crayons or markers.
2. Choose one of the flowers, and glue the photo in the center of it.
3. Tape green pipe cleaners to the backs of the flowers to create stems.
4. Decorate a whole sheet of card stock with crayons or markers.
5. Roll the piece of card stock into a funnel shape, and secure with clear tape.
6. Place the flowers inside the card stock funnel to create a beautiful bouquet. Be sure the photo is clearly visible.

Helpful Hints

■ Use a large flower-shaped cookie cutter as a pattern for creating the flower shapes.
■ Instead of card stock, use index cards, poster board, or cardboard scraps for the flowers.

Variation

■ To create a personalized bouquet, decorate four flowers, place the photo on one of the flowers and, in the middle of the other three, write a letter of the recipient's name or her initials. For example, write "MOM" or "DAD" or a simple greeting such as "HI."

Portable Vase

A cardboard tube becomes a unique flower holder.

Before Beginning

Turn the paper cup over, and cut a hole in the bottom, just large enough for the tube section to fit through. Leaving the cup upside down, slide the tube into the cup until the end of the tube is flush with the rim of the cup. Secure the tube to the cup with glue, if necessary. Close the end of the tube by stapling it together. This will keep the flowers from sliding through the bottom of the vase.

Make Your Great Gift

1. Decorate the tube and base using several colors of paint and a foam paintbrush.
2. Using the hole punch, make two holes along the top edge of the tube.
3. Tie each end of a piece of yarn to the holes in the tube to create a handle for the vase.
4. Place fresh flowers, dried flowers, or child-made flowers inside the vase.

Seasonal Suggestions

- Use holiday paint colors to create a seasonal vase. Metallic paint colors make a festive winter holiday gift.
- Seasonal collage materials or stickers can also be added once the paint is dry.

Materials

paper party cup, 8 or 9 oz.

cardboard wrapping paper tube, cut into a 7" section

glue

paint

foam paintbrush

hole punch

yarn

stapler

A Sticky Flower Arrangement

Floral stickers turn craft sticks and a plastic pot into a sensational centerpiece.

Materials

small plastic flowerpot

Styrofoam piece that fits inside the flowerpot

flower stickers

craft sticks

seasonal wire garland

Make Your Great Gift

1. Place the Styrofoam inside the flowerpot.
2. Use flower stickers to decorate the outside of the pot.
3. Place a flower sticker on one end of each craft stick.
4. Stick the plain end of each craft stick into the Styrofoam inside the flowerpot to create a flower arrangement.
5. Use the seasonal wire garland to wind among the craft stick flowers.

Variation

- Instead of placing stickers on the ends of the craft sticks, glue paper flowers to the sticks. Use markers or collage materials to decorate the flowers.

Seasonal Suggestions

- Create an arrangement for a festive occasion by using appropriate stickers and paper shapes. For a winter holiday, use shiny star or bell stickers.
- Use a nontoxic permanent marker to write a holiday greeting on the side of the flowerpot.

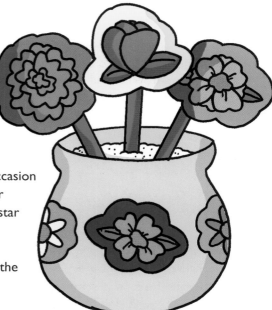

Garden Marker

Use a wooden paint stick and a plastic lid to add color to the yard or garden.

Before Beginning

Cover the printed side of the lid with contact paper. Cut two horizontal slits in the lid, approximately ½" inch apart.

Make Your Great Gift

1. Decorate the paint stir stick with the craft foam pieces.
2. Use the craft foam to decorate the side of the lid covered with contact paper.
3. On the blank side of the lid, use the permanent marker to write a title or greeting such as "Grandma's Garden" or "Welcome."
4. Slide the lid onto the stick through the horizontal slits in the lid. Position the lid so that it is at the top end of the stick and the printed greeting is visible.

Seasonal Suggestions

- Gardens are associated with springtime, making this a great Mother's Day gift. Tie a packet of inexpensive flower seeds to the garden marker, along with a copy of the following poem:

  Roses are red, and violets are blue.
  I think you are terrific.
  Happy Mother's Day to you!

- Self-adhesive foam can be purchased at most craft, fabric, and discount stores in a variety of bright, seasonal colors. Consider cutting the foam into shapes, such as hearts or flowers, or purchasing precut seasonal shapes and letters.

Materials

plastic margarine lid

colored contact paper

scissors

wooden paint stir stick

self-adhesive craft foam, cut into small geometric shapes

nontoxic permanent marker

CHAPTER 2 A Garden of Gifts

Love Bug Plant Stake

Say "I love you" with this indoor plant decoration made from a craft stick and Styrofoam.

Materials

two wiggly eyes

pipe cleaners, cut into 3" pieces

small paper hearts

heart-shaped confetti

glue

Styrofoam ball, several inches in diameter

craft stick

ribbon

Make Your Great Gift

1. Create a "love bug" by gluing two wiggly eyes, pipe cleaners, and heart-shaped collage materials onto the Styrofoam ball.
2. After the bug is dry, push the ball onto the end of a craft stick, and secure it with a few drops of glue.
3. When the plant stake is completely dry, attach a copy of the following poem to the craft stick using ribbon:

   This little love bug is from me to you.
   She sits in your plants and carries a special message, too.
   Every time you see her watching all you do,
   She is your reminder that I love you!

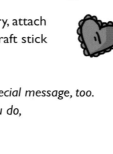

Helpful Hint

■ Make this gift extra special by placing it inside a small flowering plant.

Mini Birdbath

Plastic bottles come together to create a mini birdbath.

Before Beginning

Cut off the neck portion of one of the 2-liter clear plastic bottles that has already been cut off 5" from the top (adult only).

Make Your Great Gift

1. Decorate the outside of the cut portion with nontoxic oil pastels (or permanent markers). Add lots of color.
2. Push the decorated piece into another cut top from a 2-liter plastic bottle (with neck remaining). This will protect the oil pastel decoration.
3. Screw a plastic lid to the decorated funnel shape. Set aside.
4. Place a variety of materials into the base of the cut-off bottom portion of the 1-liter bottle. This will serve as the birdbath stand. Fill it about half full, allowing room for the birdbath top.
5. Push the decorated top, lid side down, into the base containing decorative materials. Some may have to be moved slightly so that the top sits securely.
6. Use a hot glue gun (adult only!) to fasten the pieces together. The birdbath is ready to fill with water!

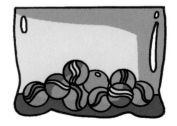

Helpful Hints

- Use sandpaper to sand any rough edges of plastic.
- Use remaining plastic bottle parts to make funnels for sand or water play. Use the remaining bases for making Mosaic Bottle Organizers (see page 60).
- Instead of putting water inside, fill with dirt, and plant flowers to create a unique flower pot.

Materials

two 2-liter clear plastic bottles, cut off 5" from top, with lids

one 1-liter clear plastic bottle, cut off 3" from bottom

scissors or utility knife (adult use only)

nontoxic oil pastels

decorative materials to put in the base

glue gun (adult use only)

CHAPTER 2 A Garden of Gifts

Watering Can

Gardeners will love this watering can made from a liquid laundry soap jug and markers.

Materials

liquid laundry detergent jug

sharp scissors or utility knife (adult only)

nontoxic permanent markers

hole punch

Before Beginning

Cut off the top portion of the jug, along the top ridge and just above the handle. Soak bottle in water to remove labels.

Make Your Great Gift

1. Decorate the outside of the watering can with nontoxic permanent markers. Create a colorful picture or design.
2. Fill the watering can with homemade flowers (see pages 28–30), or fill the container with dirt, and plant flowers or flower seeds inside.

Variation

■ Roll up pieces of tape, and use them to attach flat plastic stencil shapes to the outside of the watering can. Apply nontoxic permanent marker in a zigzag motion around the edge of the stencils. Remove the stencils, and add detail to the shape outlines.

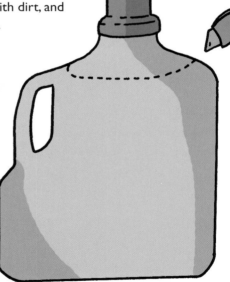

Helpful Hints

- Save cut-off tops for funnels to use in sand and water play.
- A utility knife works well for cutting off bottle tops, but be careful! (Utility knives are for adult use only.)
- Use Teflon scrapers or scrub brushes to remove residue from labels. This is fun to do outside in a tub of water.
- Use scraps of wallpaper, tissue paper, construction paper, and pipe cleaners to create a unique bouquet of flowers to place in the watering can.

Seasonal Suggestion

- Fill the can with homemade flowers for a super Mother's Day, Grandparent's Day, Teacher Appreciation Day, or May Day gift.

Terra-Cotta Music Makers

Charm a special person with beautiful chime music.

Materials

small clay pots

paint such as nontoxic outdoor acrylic craft paint

paintbrushes

clear acrylic spray (adult use only)

twine or rope, cut into 1'–2' lengths

clapper, one per pot (old earrings, metal washers, or bell)

Make Your Great Gift

1. Paint the clay pot using a brush and various colors of tempera paint.
2. After the pot dries, spray it with clear acrylic to seal the tempera paint. (This must be done outside by adults only.)
3. Allow to dry. Repeat steps 1 and 2 to make additional pots.
4. Thread twine or rope through the hole in the clay pot.
5. Tie a knot right under the hole, allowing enough twine or rope to hang out of the bottom to attach the clapper.
6. Thread the twine or rope through the clapper. Tie on the clapper, allowing it to hang freely inside the pot.
7. Tie the pots together at the top end of the twine or rope, allowing them to hang freely.

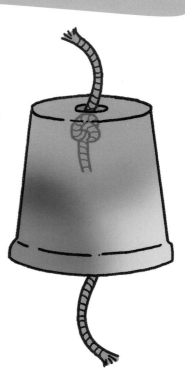

Helpful Hints

- When selecting pots, choose those that are smaller than a cup size, without any cracks or chips.
- Vary clapper types among pots to create diverse sounds.
- Paint a base coat using a sponge. When dry, paint detail with a paintbrush.
- Add details by using dark-colored, nontoxic permanent markers on top of paint and acrylic coat.

Seasonal Suggestions

■ For Mother's Day, use pastel paint to create a beautiful musical gift moms and grandmothers will enjoy. Use paint in warm, earth tones to make a Thanksgiving treasure for a loved one.

■ Make individual music makers into holiday bells or ornaments.

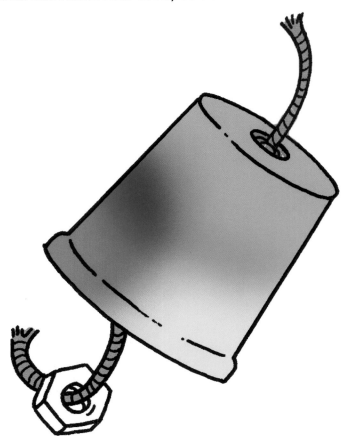

Wind Catcher

Add a splash of color with a wind catcher made from craft foam and yarn.

Materials

colored craft foam, approximately 9" x 17"

colored craft foam, cut into small shapes or prepurchased shapes

glue

ribbon, fabric strips or yarn, cut into 2' lengths

hole punch

Make Your Great Gift

1. Glue small foam shapes onto one large piece of craft foam.
2. After the glue has dried, decide where to place the holes, and use a hole punch to put holes along one long edge of the craft foam. This will be the bottom of the wind catcher.
3. String ribbon or yarn through the holes. Tie them into place so they hang freely.
4. Punch four holes along the top edge of the wind catcher at equal distances.
5. Bring short edges of the large piece of foam together to form a tube shape. Glue or staple the edges together to secure the tube.
6. Choose yarn to string through the top four holes. Thread each piece of yarn through one of the holes. Bring together the four loose ends to tie a knot. The wind catcher is ready to hang!

Helpful Hint

■ Other items that can be used to decorate the wind catcher include acrylic paint (older children), fabric scraps, felt pieces, or nontoxic permanent markers.

Seasonal Suggestion

■ For winter holidays, use glitter paint to decorate the top of a wind catcher, and substitute foil gift ribbon for the wind catcher tails. Hang in a window to reflect the light.

Come Play with Me

Share the gift of time with these great ideas that encourage family bonding.

Picture Puzzle

Make a puzzle from a photograph for a very personal gift.

Materials

glue

photo of child (may be a photocopy)

poster board or thin cardboard, cut into two 7" x 8" rectangles

markers

paper lunch sack

Make Your Great Gift

1. Glue the photo to the middle of the piece of poster board or cardboard.
2. Using markers, decorate the poster board around the photo.
3. While the glue on the poster board dries, decorate a paper lunch sack with markers.
4. After the glue is dry, cut the poster board picture into six or eight pieces. Put the picture puzzle into the lunch sack. Include the second piece of blank poster board and a note encouraging the recipient to put the picture puzzle together with you, then use the other poster board to create a puzzle together.

Helpful Hint

- Explain that the photo selected will be cut to make puzzle pieces. This may avoid an upset later on.

Seasonal Suggestions

- Before decorating the poster board square, write a brief message, such as "Happy Grandparent's Day," across the top.
- Seasonal ink stamps and washable inkpads may be used to decorate the border of the picture puzzle.

I Spy Fun

Decorated tubes turn into hours of family fun.

Make Your Great Gift

1. Decorate two 6" tubes with paint.
2. After the paint dries, glue a variety of collage materials, including wiggly eyes, to the tubes.
3. When the tubes are completely dry, place both tubes in a plastic bag along with a copy of the following poem and game instructions:

   I spy someone very special to me,
   A person who is lots of fun, too.
   Someone I like to play games with.
   And that special person is you!

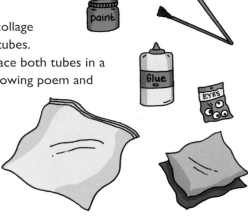

Materials

cardboard wrapping paper tube or potato chip can with ends cut off, cut into 6" sections

paint

paintbrushes

glue

collage materials

wiggly eyes

large zipper-seal plastic bag

How to Play "I Spy"

As you each look through the tubes, describe objects that you see. Talk about the colors, shapes, and sizes of the objects, and try to guess what the other person sees. Other ideas:

■ Look for objects that are a certain color or shape. For example, see how many round objects you can find in two minutes.

■ Look at each other, and describe something that the other person is wearing.

■ Look out the window, and describe items that are found outdoors.

Helpful Hint

■ Play "I Spy" with the child to give him or her a chance to learn how the game is played. This will help the child to explain the game to the recipient of the gift and to play the game successfully with the recipient.

Play-with-Me Game Box

Turn a box into a traveling game container to share with anyone, anywhere.

Materials

box with flip-top lid (e.g., shoebox, clean laundry detergent box)

sandpaper, as needed

dish soap, as needed

paint in shallow pan

small roller paintbrush

nontoxic oil pastels

games

Make Your Great Gift

1. Use sandpaper on boxes that have a glossy finish, or add a few drops of dish soap to the paint to help it adhere to the box.
2. Use a small roller paintbrush to paint the lid and sides of the box with paint.
3. Allow the paint to dry completely.
4. Decorate the top and sides of the box with nontoxic oil pastels. Personalize the box by titling it, such as "Mueller Grab-It-and-Go Game Box."
5. Fill the container with small, ready-made or homemade games. Give the box as a gift for summer family travel, a trip to the grandparents', or holiday break time.

Helpful Hint

- Spray oil pastel drawings with a light coat of hairspray to prevent smearing (adult only). Use the hairspray away from children.

Game Ideas

Tic-Tac-Toe

- Use markers to draw a Tic-Tac-Toe grid on the inside of the box lid.
- Create game pieces with juice lids or poker chips, 10 per game.
- Stick garage-sale circle dots onto the game pieces. Choose two colors, and make five game pieces of each color.
- Use nontoxic permanent markers to add features to the dots. Make creatures, people, designs, or anything else the imagination dreams up.
- Store the pieces inside the game box, sealed in a zipper-seal plastic sandwich bag.

Juice Box Memory

- Save and clean juice boxes. Cut the fronts off the boxes.
- Find matching pairs of juice-box fronts, enough to make six to nine pairs.
- To play, lay the juice-box fronts facedown, lift two at a time, and try to find a match.
- Store the pieces inside the game box, sealed in a zipper-seal plastic sandwich bag. **Option**: Collect metal juice lids or other lids and pairs of stickers. Put one sticker on each lid; use as above.

Pick-Up Sticks

- Make pick-up sticks using colorful drink stirrers or coffee stirrers.
- Play the game by holding the sticks in a single bunch on the floor and then letting go of the bunch to drop the sticks in a pile. Take turns pulling sticks out of the pile, one at a time, until one player's stick causes another stick to move. The goal is to remove sticks without causing the remaining sticks to move. Each player keeps the sticks he removes as points. Play until all the sticks are picked up.

Take-Along Art Box

Creative fun = a simple painted box and art materials.

Materials

box with lid, shoebox size or larger

zipper-seal plastic sandwich bags

art supplies, of your choice

sandpaper, as needed

paint

paintbrushes

glitter glue

Make Your Great Gift

1. Lightly sand the lid and sides of the box if it has a glossy finish.
2. Paint the top and sides of the box.
3. Use glitter glue to add simple designs and highlights.
4. While the box is drying, stuff art materials (some suggestions are paper scraps, craft foam scraps, felt scraps, yarn, ribbon, glue, markers) into zipper-seal plastic bags.
5. After the box dries, place the bagged materials inside the box, and put on the lid. Attach a note such as:

    There is a place for you in my heart.
    Can we get together and just do art?

6. The box is ready to share with someone special.

Seasonal Suggestion

■ Decorate the box in glitter paint, add a festive bow, and fill with creative art supplies that you and a parent, grandparent, or caregiver could spend time with over the winter or summer break.

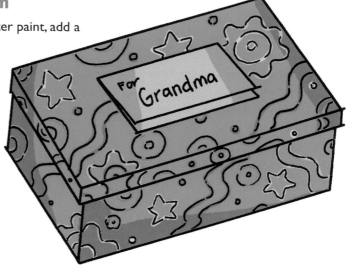

Coupon Pocket

Give someone the gift of time using homemade coupons.

Make Your Great Gift

1. Think about what kinds of activities the recipient enjoys, and what activities you and the recipient could do together. Include activities that are helpful to the recipient, as well as ideas that are recreational. Activity ideas could include:
   - cooking dinner
   - doing yard work
   - washing the car
   - going to the library
   - reading a book
   - going out for ice cream
   - making a picture for someone
   - going for a walk
2. These activities are to be done together, so be sure the wording of the coupon reflects that sentiment. For example, "This coupon is good for one evening of making dinner together."
3. Write five or six selected activities on the index cards.
4. Use markers to decorate the blank side of each coupon.
5. Decorate the library pocket using the glue and sequins.
6. Place a piece of magnetic tape on the back of the pocket, and place the coupons inside.

Seasonal Suggestion

- Consider selecting activities that are appropriate for the holiday or time of year. For example, in many places, a coupon for "help in the garden" would not be useful in the winter, but one for "help with the dishes" would be very well received.

Materials

unlined index cards,
4" x 6," cut in
half lengthwise

markers

library pocket

magnetic tape

glue

sequins

CHAPTER 3 Come Play with Me

Activity Calendar

Help a family survive a holiday or summer break with this calendar full of fun and educational activity ideas.

Materials

copies of a blank monthly calendar

construction paper, two 9" x 12" sheets

yarn

glue

markers or crayons

hole punch

Before Beginning

Make photocopies of a blank monthly calendar.

Make Your Great Gift

1. Write or type a simple activity in each blank calendar square. Activities should be ones that the family members can do together easily without special materials. Include activity ideas such as the following:
   - make dinner together
   - go to the library
   - read a favorite book
   - have a picnic
   - make playdough
   - make bubble soap, and blow bubbles
   - write a letter to a friend or relative
   - look through family photos
   - go on a nature walk
   - draw a family portrait
   - make sock puppets, and put on a puppet show
   - dance to music
   - write your own fairy tale
   - build an indoor obstacle course to crawl through
   - make an indoor tent with a sheet and chairs
   - trace each other's hands on paper
   - make binoculars out of cardboard tubes
   - play and build with empty boxes
   - make fruit salad
   - read a new book
   - act out a favorite story or nursery rhyme

- paint with water outside
- make lemonade
- hunt for bugs outside
- play Follow the Leader
- make masks from paper plates
- make leaf rubbings
- play hide-and-seek
- listen to the sounds outside, and write down what you hear

2. Glue the completed calendar to a blank piece of construction paper.
3. Use the hole punch to make a hole near the top corners of the calendar page.
4. Select one piece of construction paper, position it lengthwise, and draw a picture on it with crayons or markers.
5. Punch two holes near the bottom corners of the construction paper picture, using the holes on the calendar page as a guide.
6. Attach the picture to the calendar by laying both pages flat on a table, with the picture directly above the calendar page. Loop a short piece of yarn through one hole on each page, then repeat with the other set of holes.

Helpful Hints

- Select activities appropriate for the season and weather.
- Include pages with favorite recipes for playdough, bubble solution, and favorite snacks.
- It is okay to repeat some activities within the same month. In fact, repeating activities, such as reading a favorite book or going to the library, can be quite enjoyable.

Family Story Notebook

Encourage time together with a homemade storybook.

Materials

three-hole punch

white copier paper

clear contact paper, if desired

three-ring binder

markers or crayons

nontoxic black permanent marker

Before Beginning

Use the three-hole punch to make holes along one side of the white paper.

Make Your Great Gift

1. Think of a story, and draw pictures to make into a book using the white paper with the holes in the sides.
2. Dictate a statement or story about the pictures. Write the story along the top or bottom of the pictures using the black permanent marker.
3. Place the pages into the three-ring binder, along with 10 (or more) blank pages.
4. Decorate a white piece of paper without holes, using the markers. Write "Family Story Notebook." Many binders have a clear cover pocket in which a cover page can be inserted. If this is not the case, use clear contact paper to adhere this cover page to the front of the notebook.
5. Include a note in the front of the binder explaining that you wrote this story and that the blank paper is included so that others in the family can write a story together, or continue the one that you began. Consider placing a divider between your story and the blank pages.

Seasonal Suggestion

■ Write a story about a holiday or important family event. Then decorate the notebook cover page with markers and stickers.

"Come Cook with Me" Jar

Create a lovely gift that contains a yummy recipe.

Materials

index cards or paper

recipe

white cotton fabric

washable markers

water

paintbrushes

quart jar with lid

glue

hole punch

ribbon

Before Beginning

Type out or photocopy the recipe on page 55, and glue it to a 3" x 5" index card or a small piece of paper. Cut the fabric into 7" squares.

Make Your Great Gift

1. Decorate a piece of white fabric with washable markers. Then brush over it with water.
2. After the fabric dries, center it on the jar lid, and secure it with glue.
3. Put the dry recipe ingredients (see page 54) into the jar layer by layer.
4. Screw the lid on tightly, and tie a ribbon around the loose cloth to form a ruffled look.
5. Tie the recipe around the jar neck with ribbon by punching a hole in the card or paper and lacing the ribbon through. Put a message on the recipe card similar to the following:

   Sugar is sweet.
   Honey is too.
   I'm so happy
   When I cook with you.

6. Now your great gift is ready to send off to a loved one!

Helpful Hints

■ Recipes that lend themselves to this activity include a variety of dry ingredients (such as nuts, flour, cocoa, dry milk, chocolate chips, oats), which are put into the jar, and few "wet" ingredients, which are added by the recipient. Adjust recipe amounts to fit into the quart jar.

■ Quart canning jars work well for this activity.

Seasonal Suggestion

■ Use a recipe that corresponds to a particular holiday. Top your gift off with muslin painted with glitter paint and a recipe card decorated with glitter crayon.

Oatmeal Bar Cookies

Use to fill "Come Cook with Me" Jars.

Materials

quart glass jar (with lid)

measuring spoons and cups

bowl

spoons

wide-mouth funnel (optional)

ingredients: flour, baking soda, salt, quick oats, brown sugar, chopped nuts or chocolate chips (be aware of allergies)

Make Your Great Gift

1. Wash hands with soap and water.
2. For each quart jar, measure and mix together ¼ cup flour, ¼ teaspoon baking soda, and ¼ teaspoon salt in a bowl. Pour half of this mixture into the jar, and pack down with spoon.
3. Measure and pour in 2 cups of oats. Pack down with spoon.
4. Measure and pour in ½ cup brown sugar. Pack down with spoon.
5. Measure and pour in ¼ cup chopped nuts or chocolate chips.
6. Repeat the layers in order: the rest of the flour mix, 2 cups oats, and ½ cup brown sugar. Pack down between each added ingredient.
7. Put on the decorated lid (see "Come Cook with Me" Jar activity).
8. Attach recipe (on the following page).

Helpful Hints

- Use a wide-mouth canning funnel to help pour ingredients into the jar, or make a substitute for the wide-mouth funnel by cutting off (adult only) the top portion of a 2-liter bottle. Then cut off the bottleneck just below the base to enlarge the hole. Invert it, and use it as a funnel.
- Put the recipe on a 3" x 5" index card. Decorate by using markers and/or colored pencils.

Seasonal Suggestion

- This activity can be used for a variety of holidays and occasions by varying the recipes used. A hot chocolate mix or spiced tea mix would be great for winter holidays. A layered trail mix is great for Father's Day or for summer traveling fun.

Do-Together Oatmeal Bar Cookies

dry mix from quart jar
¼ cup butter or margarine
¼ cup white or dark corn syrup
1 teaspoon vanilla
glass mixing bowls
mixing spoon

1. Pour dry mix from jar into bowl and stir.
2. Put butter or margarine, syrup, and vanilla into another glass mixing bowl. Melt in a microwave by cooking for 15–20 seconds and stirring until liquid. This can also be done on the stovetop in a cooking pan.
3. Remove liquid mixture from the microwave and add dry ingredients. Mix thoroughly.
4. Press dough into the bottom of 9" x 13" pan.
5. Bake at 350° F for about 10 minutes or until lightly browned.
6. Remove from oven and, with metal spatula, cut into desired shape. Let cool before removing from pan.
7. Share with each other, along with a glass of milk! Yum!

Pack a Snack

Start the day off right with a healthy snack in a decorated bag.

Materials

paper lunch sack or reusable plastic container

crayons or permanent markers

notepaper

pen

snack

Make Your Great Gift

1. Draw on both sides of the lunch sack using crayons or markers. If using a reusable container, decorate with colored permanent markers.
2. Write a short note asking for a "date" that evening to do an activity together, such as read a book or go for a walk.
3. Put the snack into the sack or container, along with the note.
4. Give the sack or container to Mom, Dad, or any loved one at the beginning of a busy day.

Helpful Hints

- Prepare a simple snack food, such as trail mix.
- If the snack includes food that is messy or might melt, place it in a plastic sandwich bag before placing it inside the paper sack.
- No time to make a healthy snack? Put a piece of fruit, such as an apple, banana, or orange, in the bag.

Seasonal Suggestions

- Use holiday ink stamps and washable inkpads to decorate the sack. For a reusable container, decorate with stickers.
- Use a hole punch to make holes around the top edge of the paper sack. Weave ribbon in festive colors through the holes in the bag. For a reusable container, tie a festive ribbon around it.
- Include a holiday or special-occasion napkin with the snack.

Office Originals

Create gifts for a home or office space that are both fun and useful.

Weaving Band Pencil Holder

Not just for making potholders! Use weaving bands and plastic containers to create a colorful office organizer.

Materials

weaving bands

sturdy, plastic, open-mouth jar or cup

office supplies, such as pencils and small sticky-note pads

Before Beginning

Thoroughly clean the plastic jar.

Make Your Great Gift

1. Stretch a variety of colored weaving bands around the outside of the jar or cup to create designs.
2. Place pencils or other office supplies in the jar.

Variation

- Instead of a jar or cup, use plastic ketchup bottles. Stretch the bands around the wide base of the bottle. The narrow mouth of the bottle is perfect for flowers and creates a colorful vase. This vase can be used with the homemade flowers found on pages 28–30.

Seasonal Suggestions

- Add a special message, such as "Happy Grandparent's Day," to a sticky note, and secure it under a band on the outside of the jar.
- Holiday pencils and pens can be purchased at many educational and party-supply stores to add a festive touch to this gift.

Craft Foam Pencil Critter

Add personality to a plain pencil with craft foam.

Before Beginning

Cut two ¼" long horizontal slits in the foam shapes approximately ¾" apart.

Make Your Great Gift

1. Add details to the craft foam shape using glue, yarn, wiggly eyes, buttons, and markers.
2. Slip a pencil through the two slits in the craft foam topper.
3. Write a personal message on a thin strip of paper, and tape it to the pencil.

Helpful Hints

■ Use fabric paint or tempera paint in squeeze bottles to add features.

■ Use cookie cutters or a die-cut machine to cut out the shapes. Die-cut machines are available for use at many craft-supply stores.

Seasonal Suggestions

■ Vary the shapes to fit any occasion or season. For example, use turkey shapes for Thanksgiving. Use washable stamp pads to add fingerprint "feathers" to the turkey.

■ "Person" shapes could become a grandma or grandpa for Grandparent's Day.

Materials

colored craft foam, cut into shapes

scissors

glue

yarn

wiggly eyes and small buttons

fine-point markers

pencils, unsharpened

paper

Mosaic-Bottle Organizers

Make an organizer with tissue paper, liquid starch, and plastic bottles.

Materials

1-liter or 2-liter plastic bottles, cut at half-bottle length

dark colored tissue paper, cut in approximately 1" squares or triangles

liquid starch

thick paintbrushes

Before Beginning

Demonstrate how to create a mosaic effect on the plastic bottles by applying a coat of liquid starch and placing the tissue paper squares slightly apart from each other to create a pattern.

Make Your Great Gift

1. Create a mosaic design on the bottle, filling the sides of the bottle.
2. After the squares are slightly dry, apply a light topcoat of liquid starch, being careful not to move the design.
3. Allow the bottle to dry.
4. Fill the bottle with a gift or make several to use as office organizers.

Helpful Hints

- Sand rough edges of cut bottles with sandpaper.
- Glue several bottles to a cardboard or mat board base to use as an organizer.

Seasonal Suggestions

- Vary the colors for any holiday or occasion to create a grouping of organizers mounted on mat board. They could be used to hold cards, stamps, pens, and other supplies.
- Get ready for visiting loved ones by creating a set filled with things to do together. For example: crayons, scissors, a package of playdough, collage materials, and other art materials.

Made-It-Myself Mouse Pad

Impress a computer user with a unique mouse pad.

Materials

white or light-colored craft foam, cut into approximately 8" x 9" pieces

nontoxic permanent colored markers

clear vinyl, cut the same size and shape as craft foam

clear 2" wide book or packing tape, cut to 9" length

Make Your Great Gift

1. Brainstorm ideas to draw on the mouse pad. The following are possible ideas:
   - draw a scene for the mouse to travel through
   - trace simple shapes
   - draw a self-portrait
2. Draw the design on one side of the craft foam with the permanent markers.
3. Place a piece of tape approximately 9" long to adhere clear vinyl to craft foam along the top long edge. Then you can slide notes, memos, or photos between the vinyl and the foam.
4. Trim as needed.

Helpful Hints

- Add notes and photos under the clear vinyl.
- Clear vinyl, sold by the yard, may be found at stores that sell fabric. Or use leftover laminating film, clear page protectors, or clear report covers for the top of the mouse pad.

Seasonal Suggestions

- Make a personal mouse pad by using craft foam to put the name of the recipient on the mouse pad. This makes a great end-of-year gift for a teacher.
- Use stencils to trace and cut out a mouse pad in a seasonal shape.

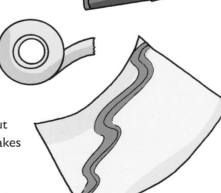

Sticky Note Magnet

Make a useful notepad magnet with a special surprise message.

Materials

poster board, cut into a 5" x 5" square

sticky notes, 3" x 3"

lightweight collage materials

glue

magnetic tape

fine-tip marker

Make Your Great Gift

1. Place a sticky note in the middle of the poster board square.
2. Glue lightweight collage materials around the edges of the poster board, avoiding the area covered by the sticky note. Suggested collage materials include tissue paper and wrapping paper scraps, confetti, small buttons, feathers, craft foam shapes, ribbon, and fabric scraps.
3. After the glue dries, compose a short message, such as "I love you, Mom!" for the person receiving the gift. Take the sticky note off of the collage, and write this message in the blank space in the middle of the poster board.
4. Stick a short stack of sticky notes on top of the dictated message. This special message will be revealed when the last sticky note is used.
5. Add a small strip of magnetic tape to the back of each corner of the poster board. The notepad can now be placed on a refrigerator or file cabinet.

Helpful Hints

■ To create a sturdier magnet, use thick cardboard from an old box instead of poster board.

■ Use a shallow dish of glue and a cotton swab to spread the glue. This will prevent saturating the small piece of poster board with too much glue.

Seasonal Suggestion

■ Write a seasonal message to be revealed when the last sticky note is used. For example, write, "I am thankful for you!" or "Happy New Year!"

Clip-to-It Board

Create a useful writing surface with a piece of cardboard, paint, and a clip.

Materials

thick cardboard, cut into 9" x 12" pieces

paint, thinned slightly with water

paintbrushes

metal bulldog clip

nontoxic permanent markers

Make Your Great Gift

1. Paint the cardboard lightly. (Don't apply too much paint because the surface should be as smooth as possible.)
2. After the surface is dry, write a message to the recipient on top of the painted area using nontoxic permanent markers. Perhaps write, "Mommy's Message Board," "Daddy's Doodles," "Mr. (Mrs.) _____'s Memos," or another appropriate message.
3. Attach the bulldog clip to the top of the finished clipboard.
4. Attach a few sheets of paper with the clip to create a useful gift for anyone.

Helpful Hints

- Masonite, available from home improvement stores, is a sturdy substitute for cardboard. Blank clipboards are also an option.
- Use paint pens to draw pictures as an alternative to using paint.
- Sponges or handprints instead of a brush can be used to apply the paint.
- Make half-sized boards to use for holding shopping or "to do" lists.

Seasonal Suggestion

- This clipboard makes a useful gift for anyone who works in an office, keeps lists at home, or needs a communication board. Personalize it with a name to make a Father's Day gift, teacher's gift, or Grandparent's Day gift.

Creative Calendar

A clear report cover and a few stickers turn a simple calendar into a desk decoration.

Materials

clear plastic report cover

seasonal stickers

computer-generated monthly calendar pages on 8½" x 11" paper

Make Your Great Gift

1. Place a piece of paper on top of the report cover, leaving only a 1" border of the cover exposed.
2. Decorate the exposed edges of the report cover with a variety of stickers.
3. Remove the paper from the top of the cover, and insert the paper monthly calendar page into the report cover. Position the calendar so that is visible through the transparent cover and is framed by the stickers.

Variation

■ Use glue and flat collage materials instead of stickers.

Corky Note Board

Make a bulletin board out of cork, cardboard, and paint.

Make Your Great Gift

1. Put a small amount of paint in each shallow dish.
2. Cut the cork to the desired size, and decorate it by making sponge prints on one side.
3. After the paint dries, glue collage materials on the cork to form a border around the edge. Allow glue to dry.
4. Glue two pieces of equal-sized cardboard on top of each other to create a strong base.
5. Construct a hanger by poking two holes close to one edge of the cardboard pieces and stringing with yarn.
6. Glue the decorated cork sheet on top of the cardboard pieces. Allow to dry.

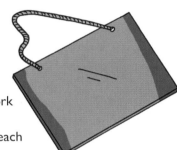

Materials

paint

shallow dishes

thin sheets of cork

two pieces of thick cardboard, cut to size of cork (see instructions)

sponge shapes

collage materials

yarn

glue

Helpful Hint

■ Rolls or sheets of cork can be found at fabric, home improvement, craft, and hobby stores.

Seasonal Suggestions

■ Cut cork into shapes that are appropriate for various gift-giving occasions. For example, a tree shape at Christmas or a leaf for fall.
■ Small, decorated pieces of cork without cardboard backing make lovely ornaments and wall hangings! Add some jewels or sequins for a unique gift.

Layer Jar Paperweight

Produce an elaborate paperweight and boredom buster.

Materials

honey

corn syrup

cooking oil

water (add food coloring if desired)

clear jar with lid

funnel

small items and glitter

glue gun (adult only)

Make Your Great Gift

1. Using the funnel, carefully pour the four liquids into the jar, one at a time. Use an equal amount of each liquid, and leave some empty space at the top of the jar. The exact quantities will depend on the size of the jar you are using. Wipe up any spills.
2. Drop a small handful of small items, such as marbles, buttons, sequins, and tiny plastic toys, into the jar. Watch what happens. Some of them will sink, some will float, and some will stop midway in the jar. Add a spoonful of glitter.
3. Secure the lid with the glue gun (adult only).
4. Tilt the jar back and forth, watching as the items float, sink and rearrange themselves.

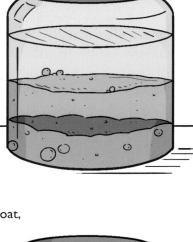

Helpful Hint

- If you are concerned about using a glass jar, substitute a clear 8 oz. water bottle with label removed.

Seasonal Suggestion

- It is easy to adapt this project to any holiday or occasion by your choice of objects and colors.

Jiffy Juice-Lid Magnet

Create a durable magnet with metal juice lids, nuts, and bolts.

Make Your Great Gift

1. Create a design by positioning the nuts, screws, and washers on a metal juice lid. Think how they can be used to create pictures (nuts for eyes, screws for mouth, and so on).
2. Glue the pieces on the juice lid.
3. When the glue is dry, secure a piece of magnetic tape to the back of the lid.

Variations

■ For added color, spray paint lids and/or some of the nuts, screws, and washers before or after they are glued together. **Caution:** An adult should always do spray painting, far away from children.

■ Other things that could be glued to the lids include colored craft foam or colored poster board petals, with a photo positioned in the middle.

Seasonal Suggestion

■ For a winter holiday gift, use three metal juice lids and nuts, screws, and washers or other materials to create a snowman. One lid becomes the head, and the other two become the body of the snowman. Secure magnetic tape to each lid. Spray paint white (adult only). Stick on any metal surface to make a snowman.

Materials

metal juice-can lids, such as from frozen orange juice

magnetic tape, cut into pieces

nuts, washers, and screws (assorted small sizes)

glue

Mat Board Magnet

Use framing scraps to create lively magnets.

Materials

scrap mat board, cut
into 2" x 3" rectangles

small buttons

cloth ribbon scraps

floral wallpaper scraps

magnetic tape, 2" strip

glue

Before Beginning

Collect scrap mat board from the local
frame shop or craft store. Cut the scraps
into 2" x 3" rectangles.

Make Your Great Gift

1. Glue the buttons, ribbon, and wallpaper on
   the mat board.
2. Place a strip of magnetic tape across the back
   of the mat board.

Variation

■ Add a bar pin to the back of
   the mat board in place of the
   magnetic tape to create a
   unique piece of jewelry.

Helpful Hints

■ If mat board is not
   readily available, use
   thick cardboard instead.
■ Select small collage
   materials that
   are lightweight.

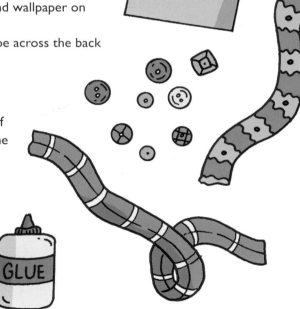

Variations

- Use paint instead of collage materials.
- The buttons and ribbon give this gift a country charm, but changing the collage materials can give the magnet a whole new look.

Seasonal Suggestions

- Glue small metal nuts to the board, and attach a note that reads, "I Am Nuts About You!" for an anytime gift!
- Use paint or a permanent marker to write a greeting on the front of the magnet, such as "Happy Birthday!"

Recycled Magnet

Reuse and recycle promotional magnets.

Materials

discarded promotional magnets

colored fine-tipped markers

card stock or construction paper, cut slightly larger than the magnet

glue

Make Your Great Gift

1. Peel the paper surface off the magnet.
2. Draw pictures and messages on the construction paper (for example, "Dad's Stuff" or "Mom's Notes").
3. Glue the picture onto the magnet.

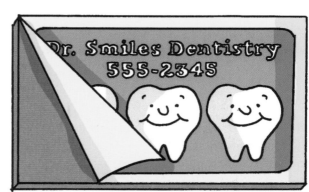

Helpful Hints

■ Other media to use on the paper cover include washable stamp pads to make fingerprints, markers to create creatures, or watercolor paints and markers to draw pictures.

■ Pictures can be laminated or covered in clear contact paper before gluing on the magnet, for added durability.

■ Put magnet inside a homemade card to give as a gift.

Family Foam Magnets

Create these magnets made from craft foam, wiggly eyes, and ribbon scraps.

Make Your Great Gift

1. Choose several craft foam people.
2. Add facial features using wiggly eyes or small buttons and nontoxic permanent markers.
3. Cut craft foam scraps into triangles, rectangles, and squares to create clothing. Glue to craft foam people.
4. Use yarn pieces and other scraps to create hair or decoration for clothing.
5. Allow foam people to dry. Attach magnetic tape to the back of each figure. Magnets hold memos, photos, or artwork!

Materials

craft foam or shelf liner, cut into people shapes

wiggly eyes or small buttons

nontoxic permanent markers

scissors

glue

yarn, ribbon, lace, and fabric scraps

magnetic tape

Helpful Hints

- Glitter glue or wallpaper scraps can be used instead of foam scraps to create clothing.
- Offer simple, cookie-cutter people shapes or stencil shapes to trace and cut.

Seasonal Suggestions

- Use brown craft foam and small buttons to create gingerbread family magnets for a winter holiday.
- Attach bar pins to back of the foam people to make jewelry.

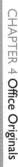

Stress Ball Sock

Turn a tube sock into a tension-release gift.

Materials

nontoxic permanent markers in a variety of colors

new, white, adult-size, knee-length athletic sock

sand

two zipper-seal plastic sandwich bags

plastic tray

masking tape

Before Beginning

Stretch the sock tight and tape it to the plastic tray.

Make Your Great Gift

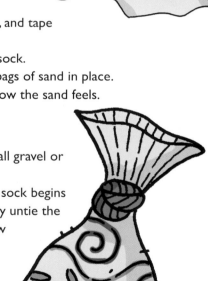

1. Draw on the sock with a variety of nontoxic permanent markers. (Protect clothing!)
2. Scoop sand into a plastic sandwich bag. Fill the bag three-quarters full.
3. Place the bag of sand inside another sandwich bag, and tape closed.
4. Place the sealed bag of sand inside the toe of the sock.
5. Tie a knot in the ankle of the sock to secure the bags of sand in place.
6. Squeeze the newly created stress ball, and enjoy how the sand feels.

Helpful Hints

- If sand is not available, other materials, such as small gravel or salt can be used instead.
- Send this gift with directions for what to do if the sock begins to leak its contents. Instruct the recipient to simply untie the sock and place the broken bag of sand inside a new sandwich bag.

Seasonal Suggestion

- The Stress Ball Sock makes a great gift for Father's Day or Teacher Appreciation Day.

Household Helps

Give practical gifts that add enjoyment to everyday activities.

Personalized Coasters

Create personalized coasters out of vinyl shelf liner and permanent markers.

Materials

light, solid-colored vinyl shelf liner, cut into 3" to 4" diameter circles

nontoxic permanent markers

Make Your Great Gift

1. Make enough vinyl circles to make a coaster for each family member or gift recipient.
2. Use the nontoxic permanent markers to decorate the circles. Perhaps add facial features to each circle, or try to make each look like the recipient of the gift.
3. "Name" each coaster. Write the name on each coaster.

Helpful Hints

■ Try permanent inkpads and small sponge shapes as a variation.

Seasonal Suggestion

■ To create a gift that is certain to cause conversations at a family celebration dinner, place the coasters inside a homemade card.

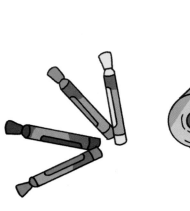

Beautiful Basket Liner

Add a touch of color to a bandana, then create a festive gift by using the bandana to line a basket or wrap up some goodies.

Before Beginning

Put paint in plastic bag(s) and seal shut. Use a different color of paint in each bag, as desired.

Make Your Great Gift

1. Place a bandana flat inside a clean pizza box.
2. Secure fabric corners to the box with tape.
3. Into the paint-filled bags, place items to roll, seal the bags, and shake to coat with paint. (Wear a paint smock.)
4. Put the paint-coated items from the bags into the pizza box containing the bandana.
5. Seal the box shut with pieces of tape and shake the box.
6. Remove the tape, and carefully remove the bandana from the box. Dry flat overnight.
7. Fold the bandana, and tie a ribbon around it to present as a gift.

Helpful Hints

- Substitute solid-colored fabric napkins, approximately 22" x 22" square, for the bandana. Fabric suggestions: cotton, nonstretch cotton/polyester, and muslin.
- Place bread, cookies, snack mix, or other items into a bandana-lined basket.
- Use the painted bandana to wrap a gift by pulling it around the gift and tying with ribbon. See the Candy Dish activity on page 80 for one gift idea.

Seasonal Suggestion

- Vary colors of fabric and paint to fit any gift-giving occasion. For example, pastel colors can be used for May Day; blue and silver for Hanukkah; or red, green, and black for Kwanzaa.

Materials

solid-colored bandana

large, clean pizza box (or any large box with a lid)

fabric paint

things that roll (golf balls, Koosh balls, or marbles)

tape

zipper-seal plastic sandwich bags

ribbon, cut into 18" to 24" lengths

CHAPTER 5 Household Helps

Chip Clip

Decorate a clothespin, and create a fun clip for sealing favorite munchies.

Materials

cardboard cut into a 2" x 3" rectangle

small stickers

markers

clothespin

glue

nontoxic permanent marker

Make Your Great Gift

1. Decorate the cardboard rectangle with stickers and markers.
2. Glue the decorated rectangle to one side of a clothespin.
3. After the glue dries, use the permanent marker to personalize the Chip Clip with the recipient's name. For example, "Dad's Chip Clip" can be written directly on the side of the clothespin or in a blank space on the decorated cardboard.

Helpful Hint

- Use other materials, such as paint and collage materials, to create a unique Chip Clip. Select flat materials such as paper and fabric scraps; materials that protrude from the clip will soon fall off with use.

Seasonal Suggestions

- Cut the cardboard into simple shapes to make it more appropriate for a specific occasion. For a fun Father's Day gift, cut the cardboard into the shape of a necktie, and glue fabric scraps from old neckties to the shape.
- The Chip Clip also makes a great gift for a summer picnic, when potato chips are especially popular. Provide appropriately colored materials to decorate the clothespin, and create the perfect picnic present.
- The Chip Clip can be placed on a small bag of homemade snacks, such as trail mix or cookies, which becomes part of the gift.

Candy Dish

Make a festive candy dish using plastic flowerpot saucers.

Materials

two 6" clear plastic flowerpot saucers

colored glue

tissue paper scraps, ribbon, colored paper scraps, and foil scraps

photo of child

sandwich bag

seasonal candy

Make Your Great Gift

1. Drizzle colored glue around the inside of one of the saucers.
2. Place ribbon, tissue paper, colored paper, and foil scraps on the glue in the saucer.
3. Place several drops of glue in the middle of the saucer, and place the photo on the glue.
4. Put the second saucer inside the decorated saucer, pressing down firmly. The second saucer creates a protective layer over the photo and decorations, while leaving these items visible in the bottom of the dish. Let the glue in the candy dish dry for at least an hour.
5. Place a handful of candies in a sandwich bag, and tie with a ribbon. Put the bag of candy into the candy dish.

Helpful Hint

■ Use only flat collage materials so that the two saucers fit together snugly.

Variation

■ Turn this candy dish into a colorful sun catcher! Use only colored tissue paper scraps to decorate the first saucer. Place the second saucer over the first, and let them dry for at least an hour. Turn the dish on its side, and make a hole in the top edge of the saucers. String yarn through the hole in the dish, and hang in a window.

Seasonal Suggestions

■ Make a Christmas or New Year's candy dish using collage materials such as shredded Mylar, foil confetti, ribbon, and wrapping-paper scraps. Select colorful peppermint candies to place in the dish.

■ A springtime dish can be made using pastel collage materials and plastic Easter grass. Place a bag of jellybeans in the dish.

Octopus Duster

Make cleaning fun with a duster made from a decorated tube sock.

Materials

large white tube socks

pillow stuffing

twine or yarn

flat jewels and buttons

glue

dowel, approximately 2' long

Before Beginning

Cut ribbed area of the sock to form eight strips, stopping halfway through the length of sock. Cut a small hole in the toe, big enough for the dowel to fit through.

Make Your Great Gift

1. Stuff the toe area of the sock with pillow stuffing.
2. Secure the sock just below the stuffed area with a piece of twine or yarn.
3. Glue jewels and buttons on for facial features and decoration. Let dry.
4. Put glue on the top part of the dowel stick, and push it into the hole on the toe end of the stuffed sock. Glue the edges of the hole to the dowel. Let dry.
5. The Octopus Duster is ready to dust away cobwebs and to clean high shelves. Include a note or poem such as the following:

    Here is an octopus just for you,
    To help with dusting that you do.
    If reaching high is the case,
    Use his legs with a happy face.

Helpful Hint

■ Substitute recycled plastic grocery bags for pillow stuffing.

Variation

■ Use ink daubers to create a polka-dotted creature.

Collage Bookmark

Create a simple, inexpensive bookmark appropriate for any special occasion.

Make Your Great Gift

1. Select a strip of construction paper.
2. Glue the flat collage materials to the construction paper strip.
3. After the glue dries, write a short message to the recipient on the back of the bookmark, including the date and your name.
4. Cover the bookmark with clear contact paper.

Seasonal Suggestion

■ A Collage Bookmark makes a great gift for special people who live far away, because it is small, lightweight, and easy to mail.

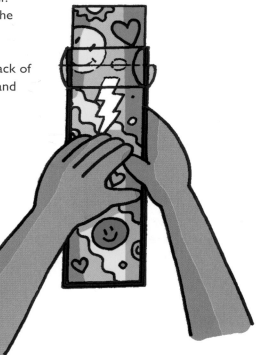

Materials

construction paper, cut into 1½" x 7" pieces

glue stick

flat collage materials such as confetti, paper scraps, wallpaper scraps, and stickers

clear contact paper

Craft Stick Bookmark

Craft sticks and craft foam make a colorful, personalized gift.

Materials

craft foam

large cookie cutter

scissors

craft foam scraps, variety of colors

glue

large craft stick

nontoxic permanent marker

pen or pencil

Before Beginning

Cut a fun shape out of craft foam. Trace around a large cookie cutter, and use scissors to cut out a simple shape such as a heart or star. The shape should be about 3" to 4" in diameter.

Make Your Great Gift

1. Decorate the larger foam shape with glue and a colorful variety of smaller craft foam scraps.
2. While the glue dries, write a short message on a craft stick to the recipient of the bookmark. For example: "I love you, Mom!" or "You're the Best!" will easily fit in the given space. Use a permanent marker.
3. Glue the foam shape to the end of the craft stick. Be sure not to cover up the greeting written on the stick.
4. On the back of the bookmark, write your name and the date using a permanent marker.

Helpful Hint

- Be sure to select a short message that will fit on the craft stick.

Seasonal Suggestions

- Packages of small craft foam pieces can be purchased at most craft stores and come in a variety of seasonal characters and shapes.
- Select shapes for specific holidays, such as a flower for a spring holiday, a candle for a winter holiday, a leaf for a fall holiday, or a tie shape for Father's Day.

"Look What I Made!" Magnet

Display children's masterpieces using a clothespin.

Before Beginning

Print "Look What I Made!" across the top edge of the index card using a permanent marker.

Make Your Great Gift

1. Glue flat, lightweight collage materials, such as wallpaper scraps and foil confetti to the index card.
2. Cover the index card with clear contact paper.
3. Attach self-adhesive Velcro to the back of the index card and to the front of the clothespin, fastening the card and pin together.
4. Place a piece of magnetic tape on the back of the clothespin.
5. Draw a picture for the recipient of the gift using the construction paper and crayons, and place it in the clip to be displayed.

Seasonal Suggestion

■ Personalize this gift by writing your name in place of the "I" in the title. Or change the title to "I Made This Just for [Person's Name]."

Look what I made!

Materials

unlined index card
permanent marker
flat collage materials
glue
clear contact paper
self-adhesive Velcro
clothespin
magnetic tape
construction paper
crayons

Write-and-Wipe Board

Turn a plastic page protector into a dry-erase board.

Materials

clear plastic page protector

thin cardboard or poster board, 8½" x 11"

white paper, 4½" x 5"

glue stick and clear tape

paper scraps and small stickers

yarn

dry-erase marker

magnetic tape, 2" strip

Make Your Great Gift

1. Place the piece of paper in the middle of the cardboard, leaving a 2" margin around the edge of the cardboard. Glue the paper in place.
2. Place wrapping and tissue paper shapes and small stickers on the exposed margin of the cardboard. Glue collage items into place. This should leave a large blank space in the middle of the page, with a decorative border around the edges.
3. Place the cardboard inside the clear page protector, and use the clear tape to seal the open end of the page protector.
4. Turn the album page lengthwise and string yarn through the binder holes on this side of the page. This will give the recipient a way to hang the wipe board.
5. Write a short message or greeting on the wipe board using the dry-erase marker.
6. Cut the magnetic tape strip in half. Place one piece on the board and the other on the dry-erase marker. Attach the marker to the top of the board using the magnetic tape.

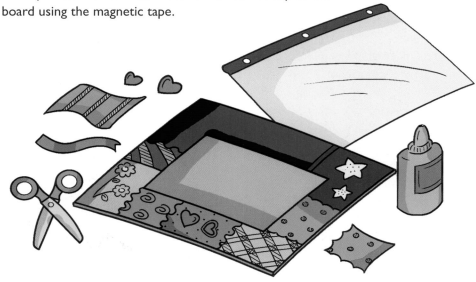

Helpful Hints

- Add one or more small photos to the collage materials along the border of the wipe board.
- Magnetic tape may be added to the back of the album page to create a magnetic wipe board for the refrigerator or a file cabinet.

French Memo Board

Turn a piece of cardboard into a handy cardholder.

Materials

sturdy cardboard, cut into a 24" x 24" heart shape

paint, several colors

foam sponge shapes

roll of ribbon, at least ½" wide

clear tape

masking tape

Before Beginning

Cut notches around the edges of the cardboard heart. Place paint in several shallow containers.

Make Your Great Gift

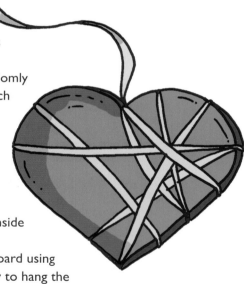

1. Decorate the cardboard heart using the foam sponge shapes and several colors of paint.
2. After the paint dries, wind the ribbon randomly around the front and back of the heart. Each time the ribbon reaches the edge of the heart, slide it into one of the notches to secure it in place.
3. Use clear tape to secure the ribbon on the back of the cardboard.
4. Write a special message on a card to the recipient of the memo board, and tuck it inside the ribbon on the board.
5. Tape a loop of ribbon to the back of the board using masking tape. This gives the recipient a way to hang the memo board.

Helpful Hints

■ It is important to use thick, sturdy cardboard for this project. Thin materials such as poster board will curl up, especially when the paint and ribbon are added.

■ If the cardboard has writing on it, use dark paint and a paintbrush to cover the cardboard completely before adding sponge prints.

Seasonal Suggestions

■ Use this gift idea for holidays when greeting cards are usually exchanged.

■ Select seasonal sponge shapes and paint colors. For example, use flower shapes for a Mother's Day board, heart shapes for a Valentine's Day board, or stars and metallic paint for a winter holiday board.

Button-Up Bulletin Board

Trim an old shirt to create a unique and useful memo board.

Materials

man's light-colored button-up shirt

thick cardboard 12" x 18"

masking tape

scissors

paint and sponge shapes

glue

buttons

ribbon or yarn

pencil and small pad of paper

Before Beginning

Thoroughly wash and dry the shirt. Place the cardboard rectangle inside the shirt, with the buttons and front shirt pocket laid evenly across the front of the cardboard. Cut out this section of the shirt, leaving 2" of extra fabric around the edges. Place the shirt piece evenly on the cardboard, and then tape the edges to the back of the cardboard using sturdy tape.

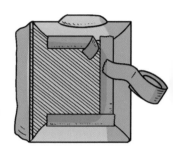

Make Your Great Gift

1. Place the paint in shallow containers.
2. Decorate the front of the shirt board using paint and sponge shapes.
3. Use buttons and glue to add more decorations.
4. When the shirt is dry, turn the board over, and use masking tape to attach a loop of ribbon or yarn to the back for easy hanging.
5. Put a pencil and a small pad of paper in the shirt pocket on the front of the memo board.
6. Consider adding a title, such as "Grandma's Memo Board" or "Nick's Mom's Notes," near the top of the board using either paint or a permanent marker.

Seasonal Suggestion

■ Write a special note to the recipient of the memo board. Write the note on colorful seasonal paper, then roll up the note, and place it in the pocket on the memo board.

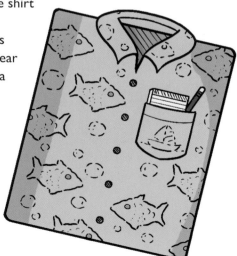

Treasure Box

Recycled shirt boxes are the perfect place to store treasures.

Make Your Great Gift

1. Paint the lid of the box, and add the gemstones and sequins with glue, leaving space at one end of the lid to write the recipient's name.
2. After the lid is dry, place it on the shirt box.
3. Personalize the treasure box by writing the name of the recipient in the blank space on the lid. Personalize the box according to the holiday; for example, write "Mommy's Treasures" if it is a Mother's Day gift.
4. This treasure box is the perfect size for storing artwork.

Helpful Hint

■ Stock up on inexpensive shirt boxes by purchasing them shortly after the Christmas holiday.

Seasonal Suggestions

■ Make a Valentine's Day treasure box by using heart-shaped sponges with red and pink paint. Then tuck a special valentine for a family member inside.

■ Make a unique treasure box for any holiday by making handprints on the box lids, and then adding collage materials.

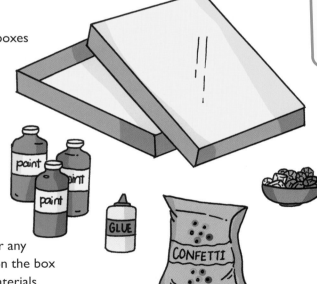

Materials

cardboard shirt box, with lid

paint

paintbrushes

plastic gemstones, sequins, or foil confetti

glue

All Smiles Key Chain

Warm a heart with a precious key chain made from poster board, ink daubers, and a photo.

Materials

poster board cut into 4" circles

washable-color ink daubers

colored pencils

hole punch

wallet-sized photo

glue stick

clear contact paper

small metal loop rings, used for key rings

Make Your Great Gift

1. Use ink daubers to put dots on one side of the poster board circles.
2. When dry, use colored pencils to create characters out of ink circles. They could be people with happy smiling faces, bugs, family members, clowns, and so on. Be creative!
3. Add a message.
4. Glue the photo onto the opposite side.
5. Trim the photo as needed.
6. Cover with contact paper.
7. Use the hole punch to make a hole into the circle. Add a metal loop ring for keys to make this cheerful key ring for someone special.

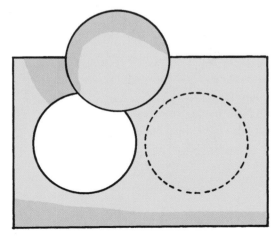

Helpful Hints

- Metal loop rings can be found at office supply stores.
- Experiment with using other materials, such as paint, to decorate the key ring. Glue sequins around the photo to add a border.

Seasonal Suggestion

- Cut the poster board into a tree shape, heart, flower, or other shape. Decorate and cover as above, then slide onto a piece of small beaded chain and close with a connector. Give as a ceiling fan pull or a holiday decoration.

Car Visor Clip

Help someone special keep his or her car organized.

Materials

clothespin, spring type

library pocket or small, sturdy mailing envelope

paint

cotton swabs or thin paintbrushes

glue

nontoxic permanent marker

Make Your Great Gift

1. Paint the clothespin and library pocket using the cotton swabs or thin paintbrushes.
2. After the paint dries, glue the library pocket to one side of the clothespin.
3. Use the permanent marker to personalize the clip by writing a title on the library pocket such as "Dad's Car Clip."
4. Include a note with the gift suggesting that the recipient clip it to the car visor and use the pocket for parking stubs or other receipts.

Helpful Hint

■ The library pocket will last longer if it is laminated or covered with clear contact paper before attaching it to the clothespin. Glue does not adhere to laminate well, so use self-adhesive Velcro to attach the pocket to the clothespin.

Variation

■ Add magnetic tape to the back of the clothespin to create a refrigerator clip that can hold papers. Use the library pocket for storing pens and pencils.
■ Use a cut-off denim jeans back pocket instead of a library pocket.

Decorations to Display

6

Add a festive touch with decorations for holidays or any day.

Nature Plaque

Glue natural objects to scrap wood to create a neat nature display.

Materials

natural items, such as small pinecones, leaves, acorns, twigs, and pebbles

wood plaque, 4" x 6"

sandpaper

glue

screw-in hook

ribbon

Make Your Great Gift

1. Go outside on a nature walk, and collect a variety of small natural items.
2. Sand all rough edges of the wood.
3. Glue the natural items on the wood plaque.
4. Attach a screw-in hook to the top of the wood piece.
5. Select a ribbon, and tie it around the hook in a bow.

Helpful Hint

- When the plaque is finished, spray clear acrylic over the natural items to preserve them (adult only).

Decorative Tile

Make a lasting picture with a piece of clay and a toothpick.

Make Your Great Gift

1. Roll out a piece of clay to approximately 3" x 4" and ½" thick.
2. Use a toothpick to etch a simple picture or design, such as a flower, fish, tree, or car, in the clay. Take care not to go all the way through the clay.
3. Allow the clay to air dry until hard.
4. Option #1: Paint the etched picture or design using thin paintbrushes and dry.
   Option #2: Roll a piece of chalk gently over the surface, avoiding the grooves, to highlight the etched picture.

Helpful Hints

- Precut the clay before beginning this activity, and keep it moist in a sealed container or large plastic bag.
- Display options:
    - Option #1—Push a paper clip into the back surface of the rolled clay before etching on front. Hang when dry.
    - Option #2—Make a hole through the top portion of the wet clay using a straw. String when dry to hang.
    - Option #3—Create a display easel by cutting a paper towel tube to approximately 1½". Cut two ½" slits on opposite sides of the top opening. This will create a stand in which to rest the tile.

Materials

self-hardening clay, neutral color

small rolling pins

toothpicks

paint

thin paintbrushes

pieces of chalk

"Sun-sational" Sun Catcher

Let the sun shine through this colorful window decoration.

Materials

clear contact paper, cut into two 6" x 6" squares

various colors of cellophane, cut into small pieces

foil confetti or sequins in a variety of colors and shapes

ribbon

plastic margarine lid

clear tape

Make Your Great Gift

1. Peel the backing off of one piece of contact paper, and position the square on the table, sticky side up. Tape the contact paper to the table to hold it in place.
2. Place the confetti and cellophane on the sticky side of the square of contact paper.
3. When the square is finished, place another square of contact paper over the first piece to seal in the materials.
4. Cut out the middle from the plastic margarine lid to create a doughnut shape.
5. Create a frame for the sun catcher by cutting the filled contact paper to fit inside the doughnut, trimming the excess contact paper from around the edges. Use clear tape to hold the contact paper inside the lid.
6. Punch a hole in the plastic, choose a color of ribbon, and tie it to the top of the lid to create a loop for hanging the sun catcher.

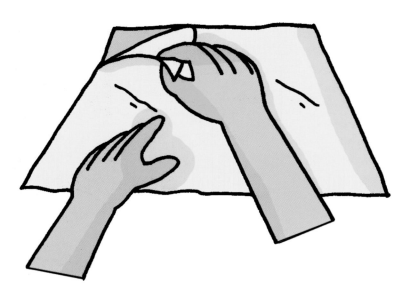

Helpful Hints

■ Use an embroidery hoop instead of a margarine lid. Secure the sun catcher inside the hoop frame with clear tape, then trim the excess contact paper.

■ Personalize this gift by adding a small photo to the middle of the sun catcher.

■ If cellophane is not available, use tissue paper or crepe paper instead.

Seasonal Suggestion

■ Try making a seasonal sun catcher by selecting specific shapes and colors of confetti and cellophane. Red and pink paper with sequin hearts are perfect for Valentine's Day; pastels and flower shapes are great for Mother's Day; and reds, browns, oranges, and yellows with leaf confetti make a beautiful autumn decoration.

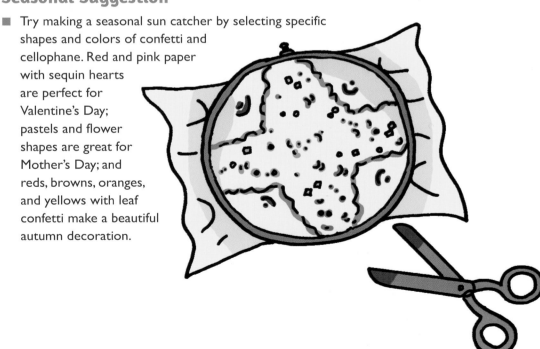

See-Through Ornament

Create a beautiful ornament to hang on a door handle, on a holiday tree, or anywhere.

Materials

clear page protector or scrap laminating film, cut into two circles

hole punch

thin ribbon

flat collage material, such as shredded paper or wrapping paper scraps

Make Your Great Gift

1. Place the two clear circles on top of one another, and use the hole punch to punch holes around the edges of both circles.
2. Lace ribbon through the holes to sew the edges of the circles together, leaving an opening at one end.
3. Fill the "pocket" with flat collage materials.
4. Lace ribbon through the remaining holes to seal the ornament closed.
5. Add a loop or ribbon for hanging the ornament.

Seasonal Suggestion

■ Cut the page protector or laminating film into a simple shape, such as a heart, star, or flower.

Seasonal Switch Plate Cover

Make a bright and colorful gift from an inexpensive switch plate cover.

Before Beginning

Cut small shapes out of the contact paper. Peel the backing off the contact-paper shapes, and stick them to the edge of a plastic tray.

Make Your Great Gift

1. Decorate the switch plate cover using the stickers and contact-paper shapes.
2. Place the decorated switch plate cover in a plastic zipper-seal sandwich bag, along with the screws or other hardware needed for installing the plate cover.

Variation

■ Add other collage materials, such as wrapping paper and wallpaper scraps, to the switch plate cover using glue.

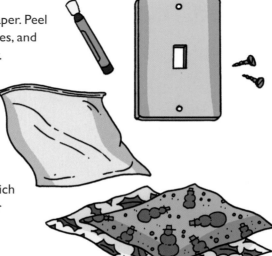

Materials

contact paper shapes in festive colors or patterns

plastic tray

plastic switch plate cover, including screws for installation

seasonal stickers

nontoxic permanent marker

zipper-seal plastic sandwich bag

CHAPTER 6 Decorations to Display

Fragrant Door Hanger

Natural items make a door decoration that smells as good as it looks.

Materials

natural items, such as leaves, flowers, pebbles, nuts, and pine needles

hole punch

zipper-seal plastic sandwich bag

cinnamon stick

colorful collage materials

ribbon

Make Your Great Gift

1. Go on a nature walk to collect small natural items.
2. Take time to look at the materials collected, and select the items to use for a door hanger.
3. Using the hole punch, make two holes in the sandwich bag, one in each of the top corners, just under the zipper seal.
4. Put the natural items, collage materials, and the cinnamon stick in the plastic bag.
5. Thread the ribbon through the holes in the bag, creating a handle large enough to hang on a doorknob.
6. Write a note that includes the following poem:

   Here's a great-smelling gift with love from me to you.
   Open it up, and hang it on your door…that's all you have to do!

7. Seal the sandwich bag, and tape the note to the outside of the bag.

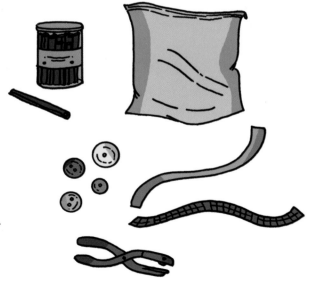

Variation

■ Instead of a plastic bag, use a paper lunch sack or clean knee-high hose. Decorate the bag or hose with stickers, markers, or paint. Roll the sides of the sack or hose down before making the holes and adding the handle. The extra layers of paper or hosiery will keep the ribbon from ripping through.

Seasonal Suggestions

■ Autumn is a great time to find natural items to be used for this gift. Dried leaves and nuts give the door hanger a harvest look that is perfect for fall holidays.

■ Make this gift work for any season by using holiday collage materials such as sequins and ribbon.

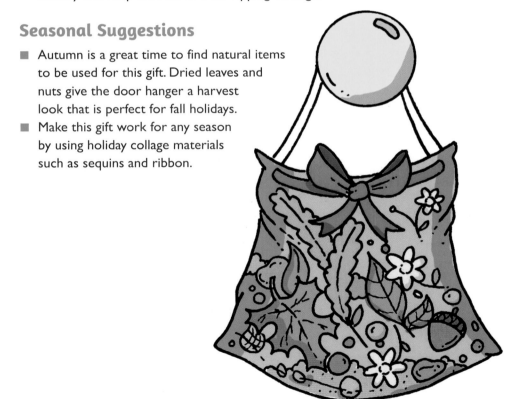

Decorative Door Hanger

Make an inexpensive and personal gift out of poster board.

Materials

white poster board, cut into a 4" x 12" rectangle

crayons

photo of child, trimmed

glue

permanent marker

clear contact paper

Before Beginning

Cut a 3" circle near one end of the poster board. Cut a slit from the circular hole to the closest end of the poster board. The poster board should now resemble a hotel-room door hanger. Make sure this hole fits around a standard-size doorknob.

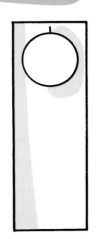

Make Your Great Gift

1. Decorate the door hanger with crayons.
2. Glue the photo to the door hanger.
3. Use the permanent marker to write your name and the date on the back of the hanger. A special message such as "Hannah's Dad Lives Here" or "Happy Mother's Day" may be added to the front of the door hanger.
4. Cover the door hanger with clear contact paper, trimming away the contact paper from the hole near the top.

Helpful Hint

■ In place of clear contact paper, try laminating the door hanger. Laminating will strengthen it and give the door hanger a smooth and clear finish.

Seasonal Suggestion

■ Glue flat collage materials in a variety of shapes and colors to the door hanger. Material ideas include foil confetti, wrapping paper scraps, ribbon, construction paper scraps, tissue paper scraps, and stickers.

Pictures on My Window

Create a window decoration using transparent vinyl and permanent markers.

Make Your Great Gift

1. Trace a chosen shape onto the piece of vinyl using a permanent marker.
2. Cut out the shape.
3. Decorate the vinyl using the nontoxic permanent markers and/or paint pens. Use many colors to create a picture or design.
4. See-through pictures need to remain flat as they are wrapped and delivered. Then they are ready to shine through when stuck to a window or mirror.

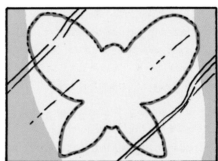

Helpful Hints

- Vinyl can be found in fabric and department stores by the yard.
- Substitute transparent colored vinyl for clear vinyl.

Seasonal Suggestions

- Designs, shapes, and colors can be modified for many different holidays and gift-giving occasions.
- A picture drawn on a simple square piece of vinyl would be a treasure for a grandparent on Grandparent's Day.

Materials

clear vinyl, cut into approximately 5" x 7" piece or smaller

nontoxic permanent colored markers and/or paint pens

stencils

scissors

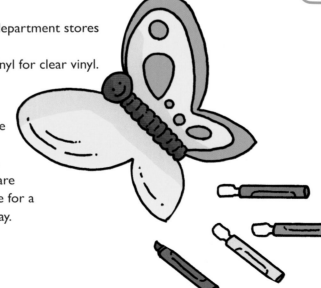

CHAPTER 6 Decorations to Display

Colorful Wall Hanging

Create a unique and long-lasting picture using fabric, a frame, and oil pastels.

Materials

muslin or other cotton fabric (beige or white)

scissors

nontoxic oil pastels

food coloring

paintbrushes

small frames, glass removed

string or yarn

clear tape

Before Beginning

Precut fabric 2" wider than the frames purchased. Put a few drops of food coloring into a bowl of water for each color desired.

Make Your Great Gift

1. Draw a picture or design on the fabric using oil pastels.
2. Paint over the top of the picture using the food coloring—water mixture.
3. Allow fabric to dry.
4. Pull the fabric tightly around the frame's cardboard insert or backing. Tape edges of the fabric to the back of the frame backing. Then, place the fabric-covered backing into the frame and secure with tape, if needed.
5. Trim excess fabric from edges.
6. Tape a loop of string to the back of the frame to form hanger.

Helpful Hints

- Test oil pastels on fabric before using to be sure they will adhere to the fabric.
- Substitute bold colors of watercolor paint for the oil pastels. It will create a tie-dye effect. Detail can be added with nontoxic permanent markers.
- Pictures drawn on thin fabric and placed in small frames can be hung in the window. The drawings will stand out as the sun shines through.
- Add a little diluted glitter paint instead of the food coloring–water mixture over the top of the picture.

Seasonal Suggestion

- The smallest frames can be used to create ornaments for winter holidays.

"Happy Holidays" Wreath

This wreath will be the perfect addition to any holiday décor.

Materials

cardboard or poster board cut into a 12" doughnut shape

seasonal collage materials

glue

ribbon

tape

Make Your Great Gift

1. Write a holiday greeting on the back of the wreath. Include your name and the date.
2. Glue seasonal collage materials on the front of the cardboard wreath shape.
3. After the wreath dries, tie a bow using wide ribbon, and attach it to the front of the wreath.
4. Create a loop using thin ribbon, and secure it with tape to the back of the top of the wreath. This will enable the recipient to hang the wreath.

Seasonal Suggestions

- Try the following seasonal ideas:
    - For spring holidays: pastel ribbon, pastel tissue paper, dried flowers, Easter grass, and wallpaper scraps.
    - For fall holidays: dried leaves, acorns, seeds, raffia, small squares cut from sandpaper and brown paper sacks, deep colors of tissue paper and construction paper.
    - For winter holidays: shredded Mylar, pinecones, pine branches, jingle bells, metallic ribbon, foil, wrapping paper scraps, bows, and cotton balls.
- When making a wreath for a family occasion, such as a family member's birthday, put a photo of that family member on the front of the wreath.

Table Wreath

Make this wreath the center of attention at a family gathering.

Materials

Styrofoam scraps or floral foam, cut into approximately 1½" x 4" x 4" pieces (or larger if necessary)

evergreen twigs

dried flowers

round beads

small pinecones

glue

Make Your Great Gift

1. Push pieces of evergreen and dried flowers into the Styrofoam. Fill in the space around the sides and top edge of the Styrofoam, but leave a clear, undecorated area in the center of the top of the piece of Styrofoam.
2. Push pinecones into the evergreen and flowers.
3. Glue beads and other decorations randomly around the wreath.

Helpful Hints

- Twist pipe cleaners around a pencil, then remove and push the coiled pipe cleaners into Styrofoam. Slide on a couple of beads.
- Cut pieces of wire garland to twist and push into Styrofoam.
- Glue unscented potpourri pieces directly onto Styrofoam.
- Experiment with making dried flowers by hanging small flowers with long stems upside down in a sunny area.

Seasonal Suggestion

- Create an autumn wreath using bits of straw, acorns, pinecones, dried leaves, dried wheat, and other appropriate materials glued onto Styrofoam.

Etched Candle

Jazz up a plain candle with a creative etched design.

Make Your Great Gift

1. Etch the sides of a candle with the handle end of a paintbrush.
2. Create simple designs and shapes, such as dots, stripes, circles, and so on.
3. Brush off loose pieces of wax.
4. Wrap the candle in a square piece of netting or tissue paper and tie with yarn.

Helpful Hints

■ Retrace over the design several times to make it more visible.

■ Use a comb to etch in a design.

Materials

votive size or other small, thick candles, colored if possible

thin paintbrushes or wooden cooking skewers

netting or tissue paper, cut in approximately 8" squares

yarn, cut into 8" pieces

Beaded Candle

Add charm to a plain candle with beaded studs.

Materials

small candles

self-adhesive gems

Make Your Great Gift

1. Peel the film off the adhesive backing on the gems.
2. Stick the gems onto the sides of the candle. Cover all sides, avoiding the top and bottom of the candle.

Helpful Hints

- Use the jewels to make a pattern on the candle.
- Add discarded small pierced earrings to the designs by tapping them into the candles with small plastic hammers.

Seasonal Suggestion

- This gift idea can be used for a variety of gift-giving occasions. A red candle with heart-shaped gems could be a gift for Valentine's Day, or a thick taper candle with small gems could be used as part of a wreath created for a fall or winter occasion.

Colorful Candle

Enhance ordinary candles with melted crayons.

Make Your Great Gift

1. Remove paper from old crayons, and sort them by color.
2. Sort crayons into a muffin tin.
3. Place the muffin tin on the warming tray. Plug in, and heat to liquefy the crayons (adult only).
4. Use cotton swabs to decorate the candles by dipping the swabs into melted crayon and then brushing them quickly on the candle.

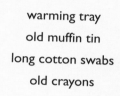

Materials

candles, solid color, any size

warming tray

old muffin tin

long cotton swabs

old crayons

Helpful Hints

■ Before using the warming tray, discuss safety precautions: Avoid touching the warming tray, muffin tin, and liquid crayons.
■ Crayon melters can be used instead of a muffin tin and warming tray.
■ Put paper muffin liners in the muffin tin before melting crayons, to make cleanup easier.
■ Put decorated candle in homemade Stained Glass Candleholder (see page 114).

Seasonal Suggestions

■ Use glitter crayons to decorate candles for winter holidays.
■ Create a Thanksgiving centerpiece candle using browns, berry colors, and other dark-colored crayons.

CHAPTER 6 Decorations to Display

Stained Glass Candleholder

Create a candleholder using a small glass votive holder or jar, liquid starch, and tissue paper.

Materials

colored crepe paper or streamers

scissors

small glass votive holder(s)

liquid starch or diluted white glue

paintbrushes

aluminum foil or plastic tray

Make Your Great Gift

1. Tear or cut crepe paper into small pieces.
2. Paint liquid starch onto the votive holder, stick on crepe paper, and then apply another coat of starch over the top to adhere the loose ends.
3. Overlap the crepe paper over the sides of the votive holder to cover it completely.
4. Place the votive holder on a nonpaper surface, such as aluminum foil or a plastic tray to dry. Or, after drying slightly, place the votive holder in a closed sandwich bag containing glitter, and roll it gently on the floor. Remove to dry.

Helpful Hints

■ Small glass jars, such as baby-food jars, can be used in place of votive holders.
■ Save tissue paper from gifts to use in this project as a substitute for crepe paper.
■ Drop in a votive candle, such as one made in the Colorful Candles activity (page 113) to complete this luminous gift.

Seasonal Suggestion

■ Obtain printed tissue paper or crepe paper that corresponds with the gift-giving occasion. For example, a cake and party print for a birthday or a black-and-orange pumpkin print for Halloween.

Beaded Ornament

Children love creating colorful decorations with pipe cleaners and beads.

Make Your Great Gift

1. Secure one end of the pipe cleaner by bending it slightly to prevent the beads from sliding off.
2. Slide beads onto the straight end of the pipe cleaner.
3. Create patterns with the beads. Secure the end by bending it in slightly when finished.
4. Attach the ends of the pipe cleaner together to form a circle. Then twist and bend the circle together to form a colorful sculpture.
5. Hang the beaded sculpture on a window latch or on a suction hook, and place in a window.

Helpful Hint

- Make two or more strings of beads, form them into circles, and twist them together to create a variety of shapes.

Seasonal Suggestion

- Use colored beads and shapes that correspond to an occasion, to vary the gift-giving opportunities. For example, use white, pink, and red beads for Valentine's Day or pretty pastels for Mother's Day.

Materials

beads with large holes, colored/transparent

pipe cleaners

small suction cups with hooks

Cinnamon Family

Give a sweet-smelling and eye-pleasing gift!

Materials

8 oz. ground cinnamon

1 cup flour

6–8 oz. water

mixing bowl

rolling pin

people-shaped cookie cutters

wax paper

white paint

toothpicks

thin ribbon or string

Before Beginning

Pour cinnamon in a bowl to prevent cinnamon "dust" from spreading to the eyes. Supervise closely as cinnamon can irritate the eyes and skin.

Make Your Great Gift

1. Add flour to cinnamon and mix.
2. Gradually add the water, starting with approximately 4 oz. Stir the mix.
3. Add the remaining water until a smooth dough ball forms. (You may not need all 8 oz of water.)
4. Sprinkle a little cinnamon on a piece of wax paper, and place all or a small portion of the dough on top.
5. Sprinkle more cinnamon on top, particularly if the dough is sticky. Cover with another layer of wax paper.
6. Flatten the dough to approximately ½" thick, using a rolling pin. If the dough is still sticky, sprinkle on more cinnamon, and roll again.
7. Remove the top layer of wax paper. Cut out the shapes using people-shaped cookie cutters.

8. Make a hole in the top of each cinnamon person using a toothpick.
9. Allow cinnamon people to air dry on wax paper. It may take 24 to 48 hours.
10. After cinnamon people are dry, draw features on them using a toothpick or cotton swab dipped in white paint to make dots, lines, and squiggles.
11. Thread string or ribbon through each cinnamon person and tie. They can be displayed individually or together as a "family" on one long piece of ribbon.

Helpful Hints

■ Wash hands thoroughly after handling dough to avoid skin irritation.
■ Use other colors of paint to add more features.

Jazzy Jigsaw Pin

Give a lovely pin created with tagboard, a bar pin, and paint.

Materials

small cardboard jigsaw pieces (purchased or from old puzzles)

tagboard or poster board

scissors

glue

thin paintbrushes

paint

bar pins

glitter in a zipper-seal bag

Make Your Great Gift

1. Choose several jigsaw puzzle pieces.
2. Paint the unprinted side of the puzzle pieces.
3. After the paint dries, glue the puzzle pieces on tagboard cut into interesting shapes. Let dry.
4. If desired, apply a thin layer of glue over parts of the painted pin. Drop the pin into a zipper-seal sandwich bag containing glitter. Seal, shake, and remove. Let dry.
5. When pin is completely dry, secure the bar pin to the back. If the bar pin is not a self-adhesive one, use glue to secure it to the tagboard.

Helpful Hint

■ Add or substitute colored toothpicks, small wooden shapes, cut drinking straws, or beads as pin decorations.

Seasonal Suggestions

■ Cut out tagboard backing into shapes to reflect various holidays or special occasions. For example, cut out a tree, snowflake, or star for winter holidays.

■ Cut several tagboard pieces in the shape of a turkey; decorate with dried corn kernels or pinecones as described above. Instead of making a pin, attach the tagboard turkeys to rectangle-shaped pieces of tagboard to use as place cards for Thanksgiving. Make as many as needed.

Say It with a Card

Create unique cards and stationery.

A "Hand-y" Card

Trace a child's hand to create a quick, easy notecard.

Materials

construction paper, 9" x 12" sheet

crayons or markers

scissors

Make Your Great Gift

1. Fold the construction paper in half to create a 9" x 6" rectangular card.
2. Place your hand on the paper, with the thumb positioned next to the fold in the paper.
3. Trace around your hand using a crayon or a marker.
4. Cut out the hand shape, leaving the fold along the outside of the thumb intact.
5. Decorate the hand-shaped card with crayons and markers.
6. Write a short message inside the card to the recipient.

Seasonal Suggestions

■ Make several cards to send to family members or friends who live far away.
■ Brighten the day of someone who lives in a nursing home with your "hand-y" greeting card.

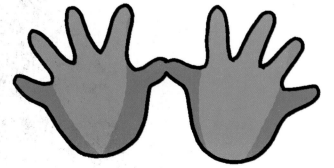

Painted Postcards

Use watercolors and card stock to create simple postcards that are almost too pretty to use.

Before Beginning

Using a black pen and ruler, draw postcard address lines on one side of each piece of card stock.

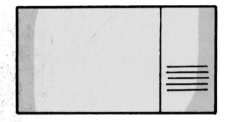

Make Your Great Gift

1. Paint each card on the side without the lines.
2. After they dry, stack the cards and tie a ribbon around the stack.

Helpful Hint

■ If possible, use the address lines on a commercially made postcard as a master copy, then run each piece of card stock through a copy machine.

Seasonal Suggestion

■ Make seasonal shapes from construction paper, such as a leaf shape for Thanksgiving. Write a holiday greeting to the recipient of the postcards on the seasonal shape, and slip the note under the tied ribbon.

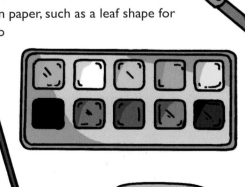

Materials

white or pastel card stock, cut into 4"x 6" rectangles

black pen

ruler

watercolor paints

thin paintbrush

ribbon

Foil Etched Card

Create a card worth framing with paint and foil wrapping paper.

Materials

foil wrapping paper, cut into 3½" x 4½" pieces

paint, with several drops of dish soap added

thin paintbrushes

construction paper or card stock

markers

glue

scraps of foil ribbon

foil star stickers

Make Your Great Gift

1. Paint a solid section in the middle of the piece of foil wrapping paper, leaving a border of the paper free from paint.
2. Let the painted area sit for a couple of minutes.
3. Using the handle end of a paintbrush, etch a design or drawing into the painted area, revealing the foil surface underneath.
4. While the paint is drying, fold a piece of construction paper in half to create a card.
5. Write a message and decorate the inside of the card using markers.
6. When the paint is dry, glue the foil wrapping paper to the outside front cover of the construction paper card.
7. Create a border around the edge of the card using foil star stickers and ribbon scraps.

Helpful Hints

- Use scrap foil wrapping paper left over from holidays or family festivities, instead of purchasing a full roll.
- A few drops of dish soap added to the paint will help the paint adhere to the paper.
- Glue a bow or sequins to the front of the card as substitutes for a border decoration.

Seasonal Suggestions

- This card is a great activity for winter holidays. Etch symbols related to the holidays, or create winter scenes.
- Create a valentine by using red foil paper cut in a heart shape or by etching a heart into white or pink paint.

Lacing Card

Construct a lively card with paper, fabric scraps, and poster board.

Materials

poster board, cut into desired shape

construction paper, cut into desired shape

hole punch

stencils

variety of scraps for lacing, such as thin paper ribbon, fabric ribbon, lacing string, and yarn

markers

tape

Before Beginning

Choose a shape to use for the card, such as a circle or free-form flower (see Seasonal Suggestions). Cut out the shape from the poster board. Cut out the same shape from a piece of construction paper. Save this for the card back.

Make Your Great Gift

1. Use a hole punch to put holes around the outer edge of the card.
2. Lace a variety of scrap materials in and out of the holes. Experiment by crossing over the card to create a weblike appearance. Secure the ends with tape. Set aside.
3. Write messages and draw pictures using markers on the construction paper shape.
4. Attach the laced top to the construction paper back by punching a matching hole through both in the upper left corner and by tying the pieces together with scrap ribbon or yarn.

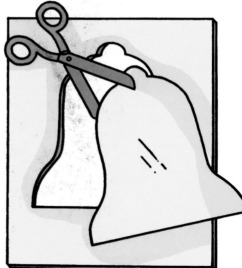

Helpful Hints

- Pipe cleaners or plastic-coated wire are good for beginning lacers.
- Wrap tape around the sewing end of yarn or ribbon to aid in lacing.
- Encourage children to cut out their own shapes.

Seasonal Suggestions

- Shapes that could be used include hearts for Valentine's Day, a pumpkin for Halloween, and stars, candles, or trees for winter holidays.
- Use colors of poster board and scraps that correspond to a holiday or festival, to vary this activity for many card-giving occasions.

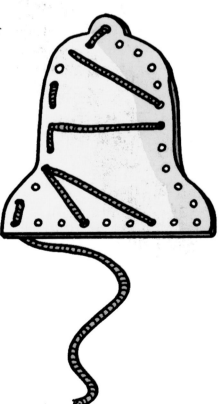

Polka-Dot Frame Card

Use pencils and paint to decorate this keepsake card.

Materials

white or pastel card stock, 8½" x 11" sheet

shallow plastic containers

sponges

unsharpened pencils with erasers

photo of child, at least 3½" x 5" in size

tape

pen

paint, various colors

Before Beginning

Prepare the frame cards by folding the card stock in half to create 8½" x 5½" cards. Cut a 3½" x 3½" square or circle in the center of the front of the card.

Make Your Great Gift

1. Place a sponge in each shallow container, and pour in a small amount of paint. Place one pencil, eraser side down in each container.
2. Use the eraser ends of the pencils dipped in paint to print dots on the front and back of the card stock.
3. After the paint dries, tape the photo on the inside of the card, positioning the picture so that it shows through the frame in the front of the card.
4. Write a special message for the intended recipient on the inside of the card.

Helpful Hints

- If card stock is not readily available, use construction paper or poster board instead.
- Washable inkpads make a wonderful, mess-free substitute for the paint in this activity.

Old Clothes Patch Card

Turn old clothing into a colorful card and conversation piece.

Make Your Great Gift

1. Fold a piece of construction paper in half to form an 8 ½" x 5 ½" piece.
2. Glue fabric scraps to the front of the card to form a design.
3. Create borders and accents by gluing on other fabric scraps.
4. After the card dries, write a greeting inside.

Helpful Hints

- Substitute card stock for construction paper to create a sturdier card.
- Cut scraps with fancy scrapbooking scissors.
- Add small buttons for variety.

Seasonal Suggestion

- For a Father's Day gift, reuse shirt pockets by cutting them off and gluing them to a card and decorating them. Slide an index card containing a special message into the pocket .

Materials

old patterned shirts, old ties or scarves, rickrack, ribbon, and other fabric scraps, cut into small shapes or pieces

construction paper

glue

colored pencils or markers

CHAPTER 7 Say It with a Card

Peekaboo Card

Make a special card with a surprise message.

Materials

construction paper, cut into a 9" x 6" heart shape

construction paper scraps

glue

construction paper, cut into a 2½" x 2½" heart shape

scissors

craft stick

pen

Make Your Great Gift

1. Decorate the larger heart shape using glue and small construction paper scraps.
2. After the glue dries, cut a 3" horizontal slit in the middle of the heart.
3. Write a short message to the recipient, such as "I love you," on one side of the smaller heart shape.
4. Glue the small heart to the end of a craft stick, with the message facing away from the stick.
5. When the glue dries, the small heart on the craft stick can be placed through the slit in the larger heart. As the craft stick moves up and down, the message on the smaller heart will appear and disappear, playing peekaboo with the recipient.

Helpful Hints

- Use other lightweight collage materials, such as wrapping paper scraps, sequins, or craft foam shapes.
- Use small amounts of glue to keep from weighing down the card.
- Card stock paper or even poster board may be used in place of the construction paper to create a sturdier card.

Seasonal Suggestions

- This heart-shaped card is an obvious choice for Valentine's Day. Choosing different messages such as "Happy Father's Day" can also make this card appropriate for other occasions.
- Change the shape of the card for use on other holidays. Try decorating a balloon shape and adding a message of "Happy Birthday!"

Handprint Blossoms

Produce a flower card that is unique and memorable, using a handprint, a pipe cleaner, and tissue paper.

Materials

paint

shallow plates or trays

white construction paper

scissors

green pipe cleaners

transparent tape

green tissue paper sheets, cut into approximately 5" squares

Make Your Great Gift

1. Place your hands on a plate or tray containing a small amount of paint. Create several handprints on the piece of white construction paper.
2. After the paint dries, trace and then cut out the handprints.
3. Attach a green pipe cleaner stem to each handprint using transparent tape.
4. Cut and tape tissue paper or wrap it around the pipe cleaner to form the leaves.
5. Messages and pictures can be put on the backs of the handprint flowers using colored pencils or markers.
6. Tie the handprints to a package or insert in a gift bag for someone special.

Helpful Hints

- Create a bunch of flowers to put in a decorated pot or to give as a bouquet.
- Use green construction paper scraps instead of tissue paper to make leaves.

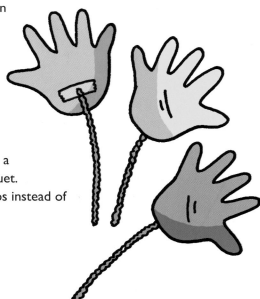

Lift-the-Flap Card

Loved ones will smile at this creative card.

Make Your Great Gift

1. Cut one large flap or a few small flaps into one piece of construction paper.
2. Tape the edges of the cut construction paper on top of the other piece of construction paper.
3. Lift the flaps, and draw pictures or write messages on the paper under each flap.
4. Decorate the rest of the card using crayons or colored pencils.

Helpful Hints

■ Use light-colored construction paper for the base of the card, to make the drawings more visible.

■ If writing a message, number the front of each flap so that the recipient opens the flaps in order.

Seasonal Suggestion

■ Seasonal stickers can be used to decorate the card.

■ Personalize the card by using small photos of child or photocopies of photos under each flap. This makes a great Grandparents' Day gift.

Materials

2 pieces of construction paper of equal sizes

clear tape

crayons or colored pencils

scissors or craft knife (adult only)

Stamped Stationery

Make simple notepaper using ink stamps.

Materials

white copier paper

washable inkpads, several colors

small seasonal ink stamps

ribbon

Make Your Great Gift

1. Decorate the edges of six pieces of paper using the ink and ink stamps.
2. Gently tie a ribbon around five pieces of the stationery.
3. Write a note to the recipient of the gift on the sixth piece of stationery. Fold this note in thirds, and slide it under the ribbon tied around the stack of notepaper.

Helpful Hint

- Place a 7½" x 10" piece of paper in the center of each 8½" x 11" piece of copy paper. This provides a frame to decorate and protect the middle of the paper from stray ink-stamp marks.

Seasonal Suggestions

- Make festive winter holiday stationery using metallic color inkpads such as gold or silver.
- Make your own ink stamps by gluing small craft foam shapes to the ends of wooden dowels or small, empty boxes.

Swirl Card

A shiny card created with corn syrup and food coloring is a delight to the eyes.

Before Beginning

Pour corn syrup into the pan until it is approximately ¼–½" deep.

Make Your Great Gift

1. Drop food coloring onto the corn syrup, using eyedroppers if necessary. Use a variety of colors.
2. Swirl the colors with the end of a dull table knife.
3. Place construction paper on top of corn syrup and food coloring mixture, then carefully lift up, allowing the excess to drip off.
4. Hang the paper to drip over a container.
5. Let dry for 24 to 48 hours.
6. Fold the paper in half to create a card.
7. Write messages and draw pictures inside the card.

Helpful Hints

- To conserve corn syrup, use a small amount in a small bread pan, and cut paper to fit.
- To remove excess corn syrup quickly, run construction paper under water for a few seconds after dipping in mixture. This will also cause colors to "swirl" together more.
- Sprinkling salt on a slightly dry picture will absorb some of the sticky texture and give the card a crystal-like appearance.

Seasonal Suggestion

- For a special Valentine card, cut paper into heart shapes, and sprinkle on heart-shaped tissue paper or confetti after dipping into the corn syrup and food coloring mixture.

Materials

light corn syrup

shallow pan

food coloring

eyedroppers

white construction paper

container to catch syrup drippings

markers

dull table knife

Woven Card

Construct a cheerful card by weaving with items such as ribbon, wrapping paper, and crepe paper.

Materials

construction paper

scissors

weaving materials, cut 12" long (choose from ribbon, wrapping paper strips, crepe paper, yarn)

tape

colored markers

glue

Make Your Great Gift

1. Fold the piece of construction paper in half lengthwise to create an 8½" x 5½" card.
2. Cut slits into construction paper, beginning on the folded edge and stopping about an inch from the outer edge. Cut wavy lines in addition to straight ones. Open the paper.
3. Weave scraps over and under slits in the paper, alternating starting points to create a woven pattern. Tape the strips on both ends.
4. Cut the white paper slightly smaller than the construction paper. Draw pictures and write messages on the piece of white paper. Glue this to the inside of the woven card.
5. After the glue dries, fold along the width of the paper to form an elaborate card for someone special.

Helpful Hints

- Create this card over several days.
- Predraw lines to follow when cutting construction paper.
- Cut wrapping paper using fancy scrapbooking scissors or cut smooth wavy lines instead of straight.

Seasonal Suggestion

- Use printed wrapping paper scraps and other scraps that correspond to a particular celebration or season, such as balloons for birthdays or foil paper for winter holidays.

Wrap It Up!

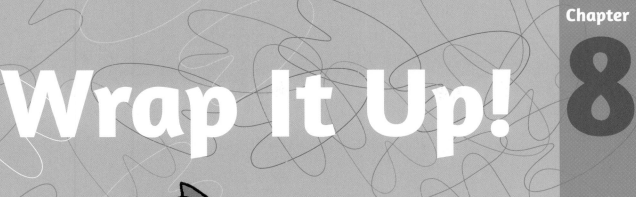

Create a variety of papers, bags, boxes, and baskets for wrapping child-made gifts.

Bubble-Wrap Paper

Create an interesting wrapping paper using bubble wrap and paint.

Materials

bubble wrap packing material

tape

paint, with a few drops of dish soap added

thick paintbrush or sponge paintbrush

newsprint, bulletin board paper, or other lightweight paper

Make Your Great Gift

1. Lay bubble wrap on trays or the surface of a table. Tape the corners of bubble wrap to the table.
2. Paint the bubble wrap using a variety of colors.
3. Lay a piece of paper over the painted area. Rub the entire paper to create a print by transferring the paint from the bubble wrap to the paper.
4. Lift up the paper carefully, and allow it to dry.
5. Use the paper to wrap a homemade gift!

Helpful Hints

- After the bubble wrap print has dried, use markers or crayons to add features and pictures to the print.
- Use various sizes of bubble wrap to create interesting designs.

Seasonal Suggestion

- Color variations lend this activity to a variety of special occasions, for example, pastel colors for spring holidays or glitter paint for winter celebrations.

Bubble Blowing Wrapping Paper

Combine bubbles and food coloring to make a lovely wrapping paper.

Before Beginning

Cover the work surface with newspaper. Fill pans with water about half full. Add food coloring, creating one color for each pan. Add several drops of liquid dish soap to each pan. Test each solution by placing one end of the straw in the mixture and blowing through the other end. Bubbles should appear over the top of the pans. If not, add more soap.

Make Your Great Gift

1. Practice blowing out of the straw. When ready, blow into colored soap solution.
2. When the bubbles rise above the mixture, lay a piece of butcher paper carefully over the top to "catch" the color.
3. Repeat the procedure for the other colors, if desired.
4. Allow the paper to dry.
5. Use crayons or nontoxic oil pastels to add designs or create pictures out of the bubble prints. When finished, it is ready to wrap up a homemade wonder.

Helpful Hints

- Put a hole near the top of each straw using a straight pin to prevent soap mixture from being sucked up into the child's mouth.
- Use an animal-shaped sponge and paint instead of crayons or oil pastels.

Materials

cake pans, 9" x 13," or jellyroll pans

water

liquid dish soap

food coloring

white butcher paper

drinking straws

newspaper

crayons or nontoxic oil pastels

Salty Wrapping Paper Sensation

Create a simple, eye-catching wrapping paper with glue, cookie cutters, and salt.

Materials

cookie cutters

glue, in a shallow pan or plate

butcher paper, colored, cut in large pieces

salt, in a bowl

plastic spoon

Make Your Great Gift

1. Dip the cookie cutter into glue. Tap it lightly on the edge of the pan to remove excess glue.
2. Place the cookie cutter onto a piece of butcher paper, creating a glue print.
3. Use a variety of cookie cutters, and cover the paper with prints.
4. Use a spoon to sprinkle the salt on the glue prints. Move the paper around to spread the salt around. Pour off extra salt.
5. After the glue dries, the paper is ready to use!

Helpful Hint

■ Pour salt into saltshakers, empty candy sprinkle containers, or glitter containers. Cover some of the holes with tape to control the amount of salt released.

Seasonal Suggestion

■ Try doing this activity on plain foil wrapping paper to add a little extra sparkle.

Wrapping Paper Bonanza

Use paint and almost anything else to create fun and fancy wrapping paper.

Before Beginning

Place the paint in shallow dishes or trays.

Make Your Great Gift

1. Dip seasonal objects in the paint, and make prints on the butcher paper.
2. After the paper dries, use it to wrap a gift. Secure the edges with clear tape.

Helpful Hints

- Use this same technique with large sheets of bulletin board paper to create tablecloths. Use paint and seasonal sponge shapes or cookie cutters to create a table covering for a family celebration.
- Before beginning this activity, select a large area where the wrapping paper can dry undisturbed.
- Matching cards can be made using the same materials and a folded piece of construction paper or card stock.

Seasonal Suggestions

- Sponge shapes and cookie cutters come in a wide variety of characters and shapes and are easy to handle while making prints on the paper. Consider other seasonal items as well:
  - Autumn holidays: leaves, craft feathers, natural objects
  - Winter holidays: plastic ornaments, pine branches, heart-shaped candy boxes
  - Spring holidays: plastic eggs, flowers, kite string
  - Summer holidays: foam balls, seashells, feet

CHAPTER 8 Wrap It Up!

Tape Print Gift Bag

Have fun while creating a unique gift bag with masking tape and paint.

Materials

painter's masking tape, variety of widths

paint

paper bag, grocery or lunch sack

scissors

thick paintbrushes

Make Your Great Gift

1. Tear off or cut strips of painter's masking tape. Create a flat design by placing the tape on the bag.
2. Completely cover the taped area with paint. Use a variety of colors in stripes or swirls.
3. After the bag dries, pull off the tape.
4. Repeat steps 1–3 on the other side of the bag, if desired.
5. Place a homemade gift inside, and cover with piece of coordinating tissue paper!

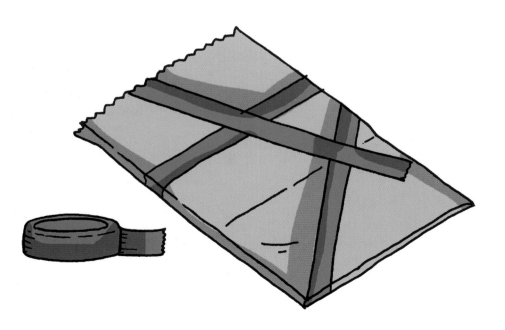

Helpful Hints

■ Precut the tape, and stick it to a tray where it can be easily removed to use.

■ Gently rub dry brushes or toothbrushes across the tape to loosen the edges and remove the tape.

■ Fasten the bag shut by punching holes through the top and tying with a piece of yarn or ribbon.

Seasonal Suggestions

■ Create star or snowflake patterns by crossing several pieces of tape at a center point. Add a glittery effect by sprinkling on salt while white or silver paint is wet.

■ Create a flower using the crossing pattern, and paint with pastel colors. After the tape is removed, place pastel colored sticker dots in the center of crossed areas to make the flower center.

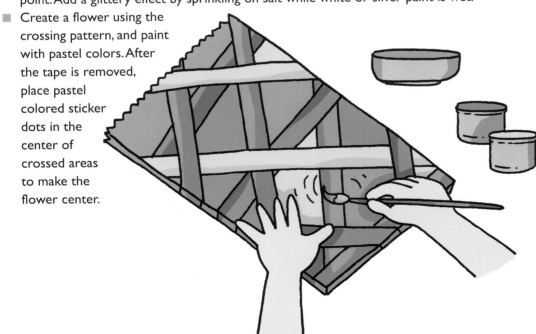

"My Feet" Gift Bag

Make a personal gift bag by tracing your foot!

Materials

white construction paper, 9" x 12" sheet

pencil

watercolor paint

thin paintbrush

yarn

scissors

Make Your Great Gift

1. Fold the construction paper in half.
2. Using a pencil, trace your foot onto one side of the folded construction paper.
3. Cut the foot shape out of the folded paper, creating two identical foot shapes.
4. Use watercolor paint to decorate one side of each of the foot shapes.
5. Place the two shapes back-to-back, with the painted sides facing out.
6. Tape or staple the sides and bottom of the foot shapes together, creating a small bag. Be sure to leave the top of the foot shapes open.
7. Punch a hole in the top of each foot shape, and string yarn through the holes to create a handle for the bag.

Helpful Hint

- Turn this gift sack into the gift! Write a short note to the recipient of the gift. Across the top of the note write, "I think you are toe-tally great!" Roll up the note and place it inside the gift bag.

Seasonal Suggestion

- This sweet gift sack is the perfect size for displaying homemade flowers. Try using it with the homemade flowers on pages 28–30.

Sponging Gift Bag

Liven up a plain brown bag for gift giving by using sponges and paint.

Materials

brown paper bag

newspaper or plastic grocery bags

sponges, cut into varied shapes

paint

salt

Make Your Great Gift

1. Stuff the brown paper bag with newspapers or plastic bags to add support when painting both sides.
2. Use sponges dipped in paint to cover the outer sides of the bag. Use various colors of paint. (Overlapping creates new colors!)
3. While the paint is wet, sprinkle on salt. Shake off excess salt.
4. Dry completely.
5. The bag is ready to hold a special gift!

Helpful Hints

■ Experiment with other things to use as painting tools, such as wadded-up newspaper or plastic grocery bags.
■ Create matching gift cards by sponge painting on one side of a 3" x 5" piece of poster board or an index card.

Seasonal Suggestions

■ When using specific colors, such as red and green for Christmas, let one color dry before adding the next.
■ Add some white "snow" paint sprinkled with salt.

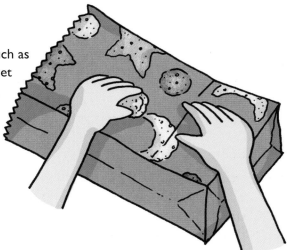

"Wrap It Up" Canister

Wrap up a special piece of artwork using a potato chip can.

Before Beginning

Cut the construction paper so that it will fit around the potato chip can.

Make Your Great Gift

1. Dip the toothbrush in the paint, then run your thumb across the bristles to splatter paint on the construction paper.
2. While the paint is drying, use crayons or markers and another piece of construction paper to make a picture for the recipient of the gift.
3. When the paint is dry, wrap the paper around the can, and secure it with glue or clear tape.
4. Roll up the picture, and place it inside the can.
5. Tie a ribbon around the can.

Helpful Hint

■ Use a cardboard wrapping paper tube instead of the can. Cut the tube in half and cover it with the decorated paper. Tape one end closed. Place a picture inside, and then secure the other end with a small piece of wrapping or construction paper and a rubber band.

Seasonal Suggestions

■ Change the canister to suit the celebration. Vary the color of the paper and paint used, and consider adding flat collage materials to the outside of the canister.

■ Put in a homemade snack or an activity idea calendar as part of the gift.

Materials

potato chip can, clean and empty

construction paper

toothbrush

paint

crayons or markers

ribbon

glue or clear tape

a drawing done by child

CHAPTER 8 Wrap It Up!

Decorative Gift Box

Recycle and rejuvenate small boxes with paint, sequins, and stickers.

Materials

small boxes with lids, such as checkbook boxes, heart-shaped candy boxes, and jewelry gift boxes

paint, variety of colors

sponges or sponge paintbrushes

glue

sequins

stickers

Make Your Great Gift

1. Paint the box lid and sides of the bottom in an up-and-down motion using a sponge. (Overlapping creates colorful surprises!)
2. After the paint dries, glue on sequins or place stickers on the box lid.
3. Place your special gift (perhaps one of the many gifts in this book) in the box to surprise a loved one.

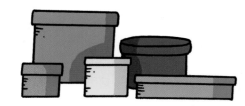

Helpful Hints

■ Add a few drops of dish detergent to the paint to help it adhere if you are using boxes with a glossy surface.

■ Using paint colors close to that of the box or darker will hide writing and labels on the surface.

■ If the bottom section of the box contains writing or pictures, it can be covered with a coat of paint.

Seasonal Suggestions

■ Heart-shaped boxes make ideal gift containers for Valentine's Day, Mother's Day, and Father's Day.

■ For a festive look, paint the box top with glue, place it in zipper-seal sandwich bag with a few tablespoons of glitter, and shake.

Papier-Mâché Gift Box

Have fun transforming a box into a work of art.

Before Beginning

Prepare papier-mâché paste using liquid starch OR two parts glue to one part water. Pour the paste into a bowl.

Make Your Great Gift

1. Tear newspaper into strips in various widths and lengths.
2. Dip the newspaper strips one at a time into the papier-mâché paste, then slide the strip through two fingers to remove excess paste.
3. Place the strips one at a time on the outer sides of the box, overlapping and filling in spaces.
4. Allow the papier-mâché surface to dry until hard to the touch.
5. Paint the outside of the box using a variety of colors.
6. After the box is dried, place a piece of tissue paper in it, and fill with a homemade gift.

Materials

papier-mâché paste (see Before Beginning)

newspaper

shoeboxes

bowl(s)

paint

thick paintbrushes

Helpful Hints

- Choose one color of paint to brush on as a surface coat. After the paint dries, paint on designs, shapes, and pictures using contrasting colors.
- Gift suggestions to put in the box:
  - Weaving Band Pencil Holder (see page 58)
  - stationery (see Chapter 7)
  - Beautiful Basket Liner (see page 77) and some homemade cookies or bread
  - "Come Cook with Me" Jar and recipe (see pages 52–55).

CHAPTER 8 Wrap It Up!

Fancy Gift Basket

Jazz up a small gift by presenting it in a basket made from a margarine tub, paint, colored wire, and markers.

Materials

small plastic containers, approximately 8 oz. (margarine, sour cream containers)

fine sandpaper, cut in quarters

paint

nontoxic permanent markers or stickers

hole punch

colored plastic-coated wire, approximately 12"

Before Beginning

Wash and dry the plastic container.

Make Your Great Gift

1. Roughen the sides of the plastic container with a piece of sandpaper. This will help the paint to adhere.
2. Paint the outside of the container, covering the sides completely. Optional: After the paint dries, use nontoxic permanent markers to add pictures or designs, or place stickers around the tub on top of the paint.
3. Punch holes on opposite sides of the tub (adult only).
4. Wrap a piece of wire around a pencil to form a "spring." Slide the wire off the pencil.
5. Push each end of the wire through a hole. Twist to secure. This creates a handle.
6. Place a piece of tissue paper in the basket, put in a gift, and it is ready to deliver.

Helpful Hints

- If lettering on the tub shows through paint, cover with another layer of paint or use thicker paint.
- One option is to sand tubs and then spray-paint them (adult only). Then decorate them with markers and stickers.
- Use pipe cleaners instead of plastic-coated wire.

Seasonal Suggestion

- Place plastic Easter grass in a pastel-colored basket for spring holiday gifts.

Paper-Plate Basket

Display homemade gifts in this beautiful basket.

Materials

small paper plate

hole punch

markers

curling ribbon, various colors, cut into 12" lengths

pipe cleaner

Before Beginning

Use the hole punch to make holes about 1" apart all the way around the edge of the paper plate.

Make Your Great Gift

1. Decorate the paper plate using markers.
2. Weave various colors of curling ribbon through the holes in the plate. When finished, secure the ends of the ribbon with clear tape.
3. Wrap the ends of a pipe cleaner through holes at opposite sides of the plate, folding the plate and creating a handle for the basket.

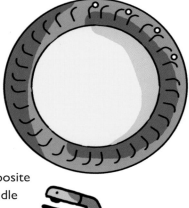

Helpful Hints

■ Decorate the plate with seasonal stickers.
■ This basket is great for displaying lightweight homemade cards and gifts. Use it to carry some of the flowers found on pages 28–30.

Seasonal Suggestions

■ Vary the colors of marker and ribbon to fit the celebration or to suit the recipient.
■ For festive winter holidays such as Christmas, Hanukkah, or New Year's Day, use foil ribbon and metallic-color crayons in place of plain curling ribbon and markers.

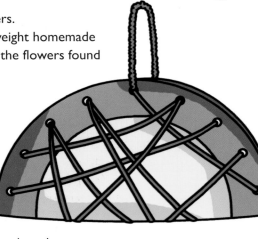

List of Common and Uncommon Holidays

JANUARY	National Hobby Month and National Braille Literacy Month (United States)
1	New Year's Day
7	Genna (Christmas—Ethiopia)
13	Anniversary of Frisbee
13	Anniversary of First Radio Broadcast
14–15	Makar Sankranti (Hindu Festival of Harvest)
17	Benjamin Franklin's Birthday
26	Australia Day (Australia)
Third Monday	Martin Luther King, Jr.'s Birthday
Fourth Wednesday	National Compliment Day (United States)
Fourth Wednesday	National School Nurse Day (United States)
Date varies	Chinese New Year
FEBRUARY	Black History Month (United States) and American Heart Month
2	Groundhog Day (United States)
5	Hank Aaron's Birthday
6	Babe Ruth's Birthday
Date varies	Arabic New Year
11	Thomas Edison's Birthday
	National Foundation Day (Japan)
12	Abraham Lincoln's Birthday
14	Valentine's Day
Date varies	President's Day (United States)
22	George Washington's Birthday
Date varies	Mardi Gras
MARCH	National Craft Month (United States) and Women's History Month (United States)
Date varies	Holi (Hindu Festival of Colors)
2	Dr. Seuss's Birthday
	National Reading Day (United States)
3	Alexander Graham Bell's Birthday
	Sportsmen's Day (Egypt)
	Hinamatsuri or Girls' Day (Japan)
6	Michelangelo's Birthday
9	Decoration Day (Liberia)

MARCH (Continued)
17 St. Patrick's Day
21 First Day of Spring (in the Northern Hemisphere)
   Human Rights Day (South Africa)
20 National Agriculture Day (United States)

APRIL Autism Awareness Month (United States) and Poetry Month (United States)
1 April Fool's Day
5 Arbor Day (Korea)
7 World Health Day
13 Thai New Year (Thailand)
   Lao New Year (Laos)
   Khmer New Year (Cambodia)
22 Earth Day
Date Varies Easter

MAY National Salad Month (United States)
1 Mother Goose Day
5 Cinco De Mayo (Mexico and United States)
   Tango-no Sekku or Boys' Day (Japan)
Second Sunday Mother's Day
8 Buddha's Birthday
   Victory in Europe Day
12 International Nurses Day
17 Día das Letras Galegas (Galician Literature Day—Spain)
18 Prayer Day (Denmark)
Last Monday Memorial Day (United States)

JUNE National Candy Month and National Rose Month (United States)
1 Children's Day (Laos)
2 Republic Day (Italy)
6 D-Day Anniversary
14 Flag Day (United States)
16 Youth Day (South Africa)
19 Women's Rights Day (Iceland)
21 First Day of Summer (in the Northern Hemisphere)
Third Sunday Father's Day

JULY National Tennis Month and National Ice Cream Month
(United States)
  1 Canada Day
  2 Ancestry Day (Haiti)
  4 Independence Day (United States)
 14 Bastille Day (France)
 15 Arbor Day (Jordan)
 20 Army Day (Mali)
 29 Parents' Day

AUGUST National Inventors' Month and National Picnic Month
(United States)
Date varies Ramadan
  3 Flag Day (Venezuela)
  6 Sisters' Day
     Independence Day (Bolivia)
 13 Left-Handers' Day (United States)
 15 Wafaa El-Nil (Flooding of the Nile Day—Egypt)
Date varies Eid al Fitr (Festival of Breaking the Fast)

SEPTEMBER Hispanic Heritage Month and International Square Dancing Month
First Monday Labor Day (United States)
  8 International Literacy Day
 11 Patriot Day (United States)
 19 Wife Appreciation Day
     Talk Like a Pirate Day
Date varies Rosh Hashanah
First Sunday after Grandparents' Day
Labor Day
 21 First Day of Autumn (in the Northern Hemisphere)
     International Day of Peace
Fourth Sunday Good Neighbor Day
 24 Heritage Day (South Africa)

OCTOBER Computer Awareness Month (United States)
  7 Frugal Fun Day
  8 National Children's Day (United States)
 10 Health-Sports Day (Japan)
 12 Columbus Day (United States)
Second Monday Thanksgiving Day (Canada)
 16 School Librarian Day (United States)

OCTOBER (Continued)
16	National Boss Day (United States)
17	Heroes Day (Jamaica)
Date varies	Diwali (Hindu and Jain Festival of Lights)
24	United Nations Day
31	Halloween

November Native American Heritage Month (United States)
1	All Saints' Day
2	All Souls' Day
11	Veterans Day (United States)
14	National Teddy Bear Day (United States)
17	World Peace Day
18	Mickey Mouse's Birthday
20	International Children's Day
Fourth Thursday	Thanksgiving (United States)

DECEMBER Read a New Book Month
6	Saint Nicholas Day
Date varies	Hanukkah
8	Bodhi Day (Buddhist Enlightenment Day)
10	Constitution Day (Thailand)
16	Anniversary of Boston Tea Party
21	First Day of Winter (in the Northern Hemisphere)
25	Christmas
26	Boxing Day (United Kingdom)
26–January 1	Kwanzaa
Date varies	Eid al Adha (Muslim Festival of Sacrifice)
31	New Year's Eve

But don't wait for a holiday or birthday! Making a gift is a great way to:

- Say thank you to Grandma for staying with you after school.
- Cheer up a friend who is sick or in the hospital.
- Brighten the day of someone in a nursing home who is feeling sad or lonely.
- Congratulate a sibling for a special accomplishment.
- Send a remembrance to family friends who are moving away.

Make the people you love smile with a gift from the heart!

Materials List

(Items that can be collected, saved, and used in the activities.)

Acrylic spray paint, clear
Aquarium gravel
Athletic socks
Baking soda
Bandana, solid color
Bar pins
Beads, colored and transparent
Bells
Black marker
Black paint
Bolts
Bowls
Boxes with lids
Brown grocery bags
Brown sugar
Bubble wrap
Bulletin board paper
Bubble packing wrap
Butcher paper, colored and white
Buttons
Cake pans
Candles, small and thick
Candy boxes
Candy-covered chocolate pieces
Cardboard tubes
Cardboard, heavy and lightweight
Cardboard boxes, all types
Cardboard shirt box

Card stock
Card stock, green
Cellophane, colored
Chalk
Chopped nuts
Cinnamon, stick and ground
Clear contact paper, clear and colored
Clear-dry glue
Clear jars, glass and plastic
Cloth scraps
Clothespins, spring type
Colored glue
Colored pencils
Colored plastic lids
Colored wire scraps
Construction paper
Cookie cutters
Cooking oil
Cooling racks
Copy machine
Cork sheets, thin
Corn syrup, light and dark
Cotton swabs
Craft foam, self-adhesive and colored
Craft sticks
Crayons
Crepe paper streamers

Cupcake liners
Dish soap
Dowel stick
Drawing done by child
Dried flowers
Dry-erase marker
Earrings
Envelopes
Evergreen twigs
Eyedroppers
Fabric paint
Fabric scraps
Felt scraps
Fine-tip markers
Floral foam
Flour
Flower petals
Flower stickers
Flowers
Foil
Foil confetti
Foil star stickers
Food coloring
Frames, wooden or plastic
Funnel
Games
Glitter
Glitter glue
Glue
Glue gun
Glue stick
Hard candy, individually wrapped

Heart-shaped confetti
Hole punch
Honey
Index cards, 4" x 6" unlined
Ink daubers
Ink pads
Ink stamps
Jewelry gift boxes
Juice can lids, metal
Key rings
Leaves
Library pocket
Liquid laundry detergent bottles, with handles
Liquid starch
Magnetic tape
Marbles
Margarine lids
Markers
Masking tape
Mat board
Measuring spoons/cups
Men's white tube socks
Metal bulldog clip
Metal washers
Mixing bowl
Monthly calendar, blank
Muffin tin
Muslin fabric

Newspaper
Notepaper
Nuts & bolts
Office supplies
Oil pastels, nontoxic
Old ties
Packing tape, clear
Paint
Paintbrushes, thick, and thin, foam
Papier-mâché paste
Paper lunch bags
Paper party cups, 8 or 9 oz., solid color
Paper plates, small
Paper scraps
Paper towel tubes
Pebbles and stones
Pencils, sharpened and unsharpened
Pens
Permanent marker, nontoxic
Photo of child
Pinecones
Pine needles
Pipe cleaners
Pipe cleaners, green
Pizza boxes, clean
Plastic bottle lids
Plastic bottles, 1 liter
Plastic bottles, 2 liter
Plastic containers, small with lids
Plastic flower pot saucers
Plastic gemstones, stick-on
Plastic jar, open-mouth

Plastic report covers, clear
Plastic switchplate covers
Plastic tray
Plates
Plexiglas frames, with or without magnets
Poster board
Poster board, green
Potato chip can
Promotional magnets
Puzzle pieces
Quart jars with lids
Quick oats
Recipe
Ribbon, curling and fabric
Ribbon scraps
Roller paintbrush, small
Rolling pins
Rope
Rubber bands
Ruler
Salt
Sand
Sandpaper
Sandwich bags, zipper-seal
Scarves, with patterns
Scissors
Scrap paper
Screw-in hooks
Screws
Self-hardening clay
Sequins
Shallow plastic containers

Shelf liners
Shells
Shirt, button-down, light color
Shirts, with patterns
Shoeboxes
Shredded Mylar
Small foam pieces
Small paper hearts
Small pebbles
Small plastic flower pots
Small plastic toys
Small sticky notes
Smocks
Snack
Spatula, metal
Sponges
Sponge paintbrush
Sponge shapes
Spoons
Stapler
Stencils
Stickers
Stick-on bows
Sticky note pads
Straws
String
Styrofoam ball
Styrofoam pieces
Suction cups, with hooks
Table knife, dull
Tagboard
Tape
Tempera paint
Thread spools
Three-hole punch
Three-ring binders
Toothpicks
Tissue paper, colored

Tube socks
Twigs
Twine
Utility knife
Vanilla
Velcro
Vinyl sheets, clear
Votive holders, glass
Wallpaper scraps
Warming tray
Washable markers
Washers
Water
Watercolor paints
Wax paper
Weaving bands
White paper
Wiggly eyes
Wire garland
Wooden beads
Wooden paint stir stick
Wooden plaque
Wrapping paper scraps
Wrapping paper tubes
Yarn
Yarn scraps

Alphabetical Index of Gifts

A

Accordion Photo Album, 24–25
Activity Calendar, 48–49
All Smiles Key Chain, 92–93

B

Beaded Candle, 112
Beaded Ornament, 115
Beautiful Basket Liner, 77
Beautiful Bow-quet, 28
Bubble Blowing Wrapping Paper, 139
Bubble-Wrap Paper, 138
Button-Up Bulletin Board, 90

C

Candy Dish, 77, 80–81
Car Visor Clip, 94
Chip Clip, 78–79
Cinnamon Family, 116–117
Classy Photo Frame, 15
Clip-to-It Board, 64–65
Collage Bookmark, 83
Colorful Candle, 113
Colorful Wall Hanging, 106–107
"Come Cook with Me" Jar, 52–55
Corky Note Board, 67
Coupon Pocket, 47
Craft Foam Pencil Critter, 59
Craft Stick Bookmark, 84
Craft Stick Picture Frame, 13
Creative Calendar, 66
Cup Photo Holder, 17

D

Decorative Door Hanger, 104
Decorative Gift Box, 148
Decorative Tile, 97

E

Easiest-Ever Photo Frame, 12
Etched-Candle, 111

F

Family Foam Magnet, 73
Family Story Notebooks, 50–51
Fancy Gift Basket, 150–151
Foil Etched Card, 122–123
Fragrant Door Hanger, 102–103
Framing with Foam, 16
French Memo Board, 88–89
Fun Frame, 14

G

Garden Marker, 33

H

Handprint Blossoms, 130
A "Hand-y" Card, 120
"Happy Holidays" Wreath, 108–109

I

I Spy Fun, 43

J

Jazzy Jigsaw Pin, 118
Jiffy Juice Lid Magnet, 69
Juice-Box Memory, 45

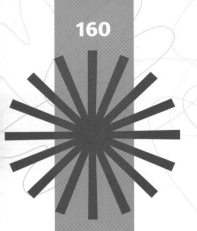

L

Lacing Card, 124–125
Layer Jar Paperweight, 68
Lift-the-Flap Card, 131
"Look What I Made!" Magnet, 85
Love Bug Plant Stake, 34

M

Made-It-Myself Mouse Pad, 61
Mat Board Magnet, 70–71
Mini Birdbath, 35
Monitor Photo Holder, 20–21
Mosaic-Bottle Organizers, 60
"My Feet" Gift Bag, 144–145
"My Year" Photo Album, 22–23

N

Nature Plaque, 96

O

Oatmeal Bar Cookies, 54–55
Octopus Duster, 82
Old Clothes Patch Card, 127

P

Pack a Snack, 56
Painted Postcards, 121
Paper Plate Basket, 152
Papier-mache Gift Box, 149
Peekaboo Card, 128–129
Personalized Coasters, 76
Photo Collage Box, 26
Pick-Up Sticks, 45
Picture Puzzle, 42
Pictures on My Window, 105
Play-with-Me Game Box, 44–45
Polka-Dot Frame Card, 126
Portable Vase, 31

R

Recycled Magnet, 72

S

Salty Wrapping Paper Sensation, 140
"Say Cheese" Flowers, 30
Seasonal Switch Plate Cover, 101
See-Though Ornament, 100
Sponging Gift Bag, 146
Stained Glass Candleholder, 114
Stamped Stationery, 132
Sticky Flower Arrangement, 32
Sticky Note Magnet, 62
Stress Ball Sock, 74
"Sun-sational" Sun Catcher, 98–99
"Sweet Treat" Flowers, 29
Swirl Card, 133

T

Table Wreath, 110
Tabletop Photo Holder, 18–19
Take-Along Art Box, 46
Tape Print Gift Bag, 142–143
Terra-Cotta Music Makers, 38–39
Tic-Tac-Toe, 45
Treasure Box, 91

W

Watering Can, 36–37
Weaving Band Pencil Holder, 58
Wind Catcher, 40
Woven Card, 134–135
"Wrap It Up" Canister, 147
Wrapping Paper Bonanza, 141
Write-and-Wipe Board, 86–87

Index

B

Bags
    brown paper, 42, 56, 103, 109, 142–143, 146
    Pack a Snack, 56
    plastic grocery, 43, 146
Balls, 77
Bandana, solid-colored, 77
Bar pins, 70, 73, 118
Baskets
    Fancy Gift Basket, 150–151
    Paper Plate Basket, 152
Beads, 16, 110, 115, 118
Bells, 38, 109
Binder, three-ring, 50
Birthdays, 71, 109, 114, 129, 135
Bookmarks
    Collage Bookmark, 83
    Craft Stick Bookmark, 84
Bottles, plastic, 35–36, 58, 60
Boxes, 132
    cardboard, all sizes, 26, 44, 46, 77, 91, 148–149
    Decorative Gift Box, 148
    Photo Collage Box, 26
    Play-with-Me Game Box, 44–45
    Take-Along Art Box, 46
    Treasure Box, 91
Bowl, 116, 149
Bows, 28, 109, 123
Bubble-wrap packing material, 138
Bulldog clip, metal, 64
Buttons, 13, 15–17, 20, 59, 68, 70–71, 73, 82, 90, 127

C

Calendars, 147
    Activity Calendar, 48–49
    blank pages, 48, 66
    Creative Calendar, 66
Candles, 111–114
    Beaded Candle, 112
    Colorful Candles, 113, 114
    Etched Candle, 111
    Stained Glass Candleholder, 114
Candy, 29, 80–81
Cardboard, 14, 22, 30, 78, 108
    boxes, all sizes, 26, 44, 46, 77, 91, 148–149
    lightweight, 12, 42, 86
    scraps, 30, 46
    thick, 64, 67, 88–90
    tubes, 17, 31, 43, 97, 147
Cards and stationery, 141, 146, 152
    Foil Etched Card, 122–123
    Handprint Blossoms, 130
    A "Hand-y" Card, 120
    Lacing Card, 124–125
    Lift-the-Flap Card, 131
    Old Clothes Patch Card, 127
    Painted Postcards, 121
    Peekaboo Card, 128–129
    Polka-Dot Frame Card, 126
    Stamped Stationery, 132, 149
    Swirl Card, 133
    Woven Card, 134–135
    Card stock, 12, 28–30, 72, 121–122, 126, 141
Ceiling fan pull, 93
Cellophane, colored, 12, 29, 98

Chalk, 97

Christmas, 28, 67, 81, 91, 146, 152

Cinnamon, stick and ground, 101, 116–117

Clapper, metal, 38

Clay, self-hardening, 18–19, 97

Clothespin, 78, 85, 94

Collage materials, 13–16, 20, 22, 29, 31–32, 43, 62, 66–67, 70–71, 80, 83, 85–86, 91, 100–104, 108, 129

Comb, 111

Confetti, 83, 133

   foil, 81, 85, 91, 98, 104

Contact paper

   clear, 12, 24, 50, 72, 83, 85, 92, 98, 104

   colored, 33, 101

Container, plastic, 56, 150

Cookie cutters, 30, 59, 84, 116, 140–141

Cork, sheets, 67

Corn syrup, 55, 68, 133

Cotton, balls and swabs, 94, 109, 94, 113, 117

Craft sticks, 13, 32, 34, 84, 128

Crayons, 14, 30, 48, 50, 56, 85, 104, 113, 120, 131, 139, 147

   melters, 113

   glitter/metallic, 25, 113, 152

Cupcake liners, 29, 113

Cups, 58

D

Decorations

   Beaded Ornament, 115

   Cinnamon Family, 116–117

   Colorful Wall Hanging, 106–107

   Decorative Door Hanger, 104

   Decorative Tile, 97

   "Happy Holidays" Wreath, 108–109

   Fragrant Door Hanger, 102–103

   Nature Plaque, 96

   Pictures on My Window, 105

   Seasonal Switch Plate Cover, 101

   See-Though Ornament, 100

   "Sun-sational" Sun Catcher, 98–99

   Table Wreath, 110

Die-cut machines, 59

Dish soap, 44, 122–123, 138–139, 148

Dowels, wooden, 82, 132

Drink/coffee stirrers, plastic, 45

Drinking straws, 139

E

Easter, 23

   grass, 81, 109, 151

Embroidery hoop, 99

Envelope, mailing, 94

Eyedroppers, 133

Eyes, wiggly, 34, 43, 59, 73

F

Fabric, 107

   cotton, 52, 106

   muslin, 106

   scraps, 16, 40, 46, 73, 78–79, 127

Father's Day, 16, 19, 54, 65, 74, 79, 84, 127, 129, 148

Felt scraps, 40

Flour, 54, 116–117

Flower seeds, 36

Flowerpot saucers, 80

Flowerpots, 32, 35

Flowers, homemade, 36, 58, 145, 152

   Beautiful Bow-quet, 28

   "Say Cheese" Flowers, 30

   Sticky Flower Arrangement, 32

   "Sweet Treat" Flowers, 29

Foam,

   craft, 16, 40, 59, 61, 69, 73, 84, 129, 131

craft, self-adhesive, 20–21, 33
floral, 110
paintbrushes, 17, 31
shelf liner, 16, 73
Foil, 14, 29
aluminum, 114
confetti, 81, 85, 91, 98, 104
scraps, 80
Food coloring, 106–107, 133, 139
Funnels, 37, 54, 68

G

Games/activities
Activity Calendar, 48–49
"Come Cook with Me" Jar, 52–55
Coupon Pocket, 47
Family Story Notebook, 50–51
I Spy Fun, 43
Juice Box Memory, 45
Pack a Snack, 56
Picture Puzzle, 42
Pick-Up Sticks, 45
Play-with-Me Game Box, 44–45
Take-Along Art Box, 46
Tic-Tac-Toe, 45
Gardening/yard gifts
Garden Marker, 33
Love Bug Plant Spikes, 34
Mini Birdbath, 35
Terra-Cotta Music Makers, 38–39
Watering Can, 36–37
Wind Catcher, 40
Gemstones, 13, 17, 67, 82, 91, 112
Gift bags
"My Feet" Gift Bag, 144–145
Sponging Gift Bag, 146
Tape Print Gift Bag, 142–143
Glitter, 68, 118, 148
glue, 15, 46, 73

Glue, 12–17, 20, 22, 24, 26, 29–32, 34–35,
40, 42, 46–48, 52, 59, 62, 66–70, 72–73,
78, 82–86, 90–92, 94, 96, 101, 104, 108,
110, 114, 118, 122, 127–128, 134, 140,
147–149
clear-drying, 15
colored, 80
glitter, 15, 46, 73
gun, 35, 68
stick, 12, 83, 86, 92
Grandparents' Day, 16, 37, 42, 58, 59, 65,
105, 131
Gravel, aquarium, 13

H

Hairspray, 44
Halloween, 21, 114, 125
Hanukkah, 15, 77, 152
Hole punch, 22, 31, 36, 40, 48–50, 52, 56,
92, 100, 102, 124, 150, 152
Honey, 68
Hook, screw-in, 96
Hose, knee-high, 103
Household décor
All Smiles Key Chain, 92–93
Beautiful Basket Liner, 77, 149
Candy Dish, 77, 80–81
Car Visor Clip, 94
Chip Clip, 78–79
Octopus Duster, 82
Personalized Coasters, 76

I

Index cards, 24, 47, 52, 85, 127, 146
Ink daubers, 82
Inkpads and stamps, 42, 56, 59, 72, 76, 92,
126, 131

J

Jars and vases, 52–53, 58, 68, 114
    "Come Cook with Me" Jar, 52–55, 149
    Portable Vase, 31
    "Wrap It Up" Canister, 147
Jewelry, 70, 73
    Jazzy Jigsaw Pin, 118
    scrap, 38, 112
Jigsaw pieces, 118
Juice can lids, metal, 20, 45, 69

K

Knives, 35–36, 131, 133
Kwanzaa, 77

L

Lace, 73
Laminating film, 61, 100
Loop rings, 92–93

M

Magnets
    Family Fun Magnet, 73
    Jiffy Juice-Lid Magnet, 69
    "Look What I Made!" Magnet, 85
    promotional, 72
    Mat Board Magnet, 70–71
    Recycled Magnet, 72
    Sticky Note Magnet, 62
    magnetic tape, 12–14, 16, 47, 62, 69–70, 73, 85–87, 94
Marbles, 68, 77
Markers, 14, 24, 29–30, 32, 42, 46–51, 54, 56, 78, 103, 120, 122, 124, 127, 130, 133–134, 147, 152
    dry-erase, 86
    fine-point, 59, 62, 72
    nontoxic permanent, 15, 33, 35–36, 38, 40, 45, 50, 61, 64, 70, 73–74, 76, 78, 84–85, 94, 101, 104–105, 107, 150
    washable, 52
Mat board, 14, 70
May Day, 37, 77
Memo/bulletin boards
    Button-Up Bulletin Board, 90
    Clip-to-It Board, 64–65
    Corky Note Board, 67
    French Memo Board, 88–89
    Write-and-Wipe Board, 86–87
Mother's Day, 12, 16, 33, 37, 39, 89, 91, 99, 104, 115, 148
Muffin tin, 113
Mylar, 23, 81, 109

N

Napkins, 56, 77
Nature, items found in, 96, 102, 109–110
Netting, 111
New Year's Day, 81, 152
Newspaper, 139, 146, 149
Nuts, metal, 69, 71

O

Oatmeal Bar Cookies, 54–55, 149
Office decorations/organizers
    Craft Foam Pencil Critter, 59
    Creative Calendar, 66
    Layer Jar Paperweight, 68
    Made-It-Myself Mouse Pad, 61
    Mosaic-Bottle Organizers, 35, 60
    Sticky-Note Magnet, 62
    Stress Ball Sock, 74
    Weaving Band Pencil Holder, 58, 149
Oil pastels, 35, 44, 106–107, 139
Oil, cooking, 68

P

Page protectors, 61, 86, 100
Paint, 17, 31, 43–44, 46, 64, 67, 70–71, 88,
    90–91, 93–94, 97, 103, 116–118, 122,
    126, 130, 138–139, 141–143, 146–150
    acrylic, 38–40
    fabric, 59, 77
    glitter/metallic, 31, 53, 107, 138
    pens, 65, 105
    spray, 38, 69, 96
    stir sticks, wooden, 33
    tempera, 18, 59
    watercolor, 72, 107, 121, 144
Paintbrushes, 18, 26, 43, 46, 52, 64, 106,
    114
    foam/sponge, 17, 31
    sponge, 17, 65, 138, 148
    roller, 44
    thin, 91, 97, 111, 118, 121–122, 144
    thick, 60, 138, 142, 149
Pans, 133, 139–140
Paper, 14, 56, 59, 94
    butcher, 138–141
    construction, 34, 37, 48–49, 72, 80,
        83, 85, 109, 120, 122, 124, 127–128,
        130–131, 133–135, 141, 144–145,
        147
    contact, 12, 24, 33, 50, 72, 83, 85, 92,
        98, 101, 104
    copier, white, 50, 86, 132
    crêpe, 114, 134
    cups, 17, 31
    lunch sacks, 42, 56, 103, 109, 142–
        143, 146
    newsprint, 138, 141
    pads, 90
    plates, 152
    scraps, 14–15, 20, 37, 46, 78, 80, 83,
        86, 100, 125, 128

tissue, 12, 28–29, 37, 60, 80, 86, 104,
    109, 111, 114, 130, 133, 150
wax, 116
Paper clips, 97
Papier-mâché paste, 149
Pens, 56, 58, 84, 121, 126, 128
Pencils, 58, 84, 90, 92, 131, 144
    colored, 24, 127, 130
    unsharpened, 59, 126
Photo albums
    Accordion Photo Album, 24–25
    "My Year" Photo Album, 22–23
Photocopies, 26, 42, 52
Photographs, 12–25, 30, 42, 61, 80, 87, 81,
    99, 104, 121, 126
Picture Frames, 106
    Classy Photo Frame, 15
    Craft Stick Picture Frame, 13
    Cup Photo Holder, 17
    Easiest-Ever Photo Frame, 12
    Framing with Foam, 16
    Fun Frame, 14
    Monitor Photo Holder, 20–21
    Tabletop Photo Holder, 18–19
Pillow stuffing, 82
Pipe cleaners, 21, 30, 34, 37, 115, 125,
    130, 151–152
Plaque, wood, 96
Plastic
    bottles, 35–36, 58, 60
    bags, 43, 146
    containers, 56, 150
    drink/coffee stirrers, 45
    gemstones, 13, 17, 67, 82, 91
    margarine lids, 33, 98
    report covers, 66
    sandwich bags, 22, 45–46, 74, 77, 80,
        101–103, 118, 148
    spoons, 140
    trays, 74, 101, 114, 126, 130

Plexiglas frame, 15
Pockets,
    library, 47, 94
    pants, 94
Poems for projects, 33–34, 43, 46, 52–53, 82, 102
Poster board, 28, 42, 62, 69, 86, 92, 104, 108, 118, 124–126, 146
Potato chip can, 147
Potpourri, 110
Pots, clay, 38

R

Recipes, 52–55, 149
Refrigerator clips, 94
Report covers, clear plastic, 66
Ribbon, 14, 16, 22, 24, 28, 34, 40, 52, 56, 73, 77, 81, 88, 90, 96, 98, 100, 102–104, 108–109, 116, 121, 124–125, 127, 131, 134, 147
    cloth, 70–71
    curling, 152
    foil, 122
    metallic, 25
Rickrack, 127
Rolling pin, 97, 116
Rope, 38
Rubber bands, 147
Ruler, 121

S

St. Patrick's Day, 28
Salt, 133, 140, 143, 146
Sand, 74
Sandpaper, 35, 44, 46, 96, 150
Sandwich bags, plastic, 22, 80
    zipper-seal, 45–46, 74, 77, 101–103, 118, 148
Scissors, 14, 16, 26, 33, 35–36, 59, 73, 84, 90, 105–106, 114, 118, 120, 128, 130–131, 134, 142–143

scrapbooking, 127
Screws, metal, 69
Sequins, 15–16, 20, 47, 67–68, 91, 98–99, 103, 123, 129, 148
Shirts, 90, 126
Skewers, wooden, 111
Socks, 74, 82
Spatula, metal, 18
Sponges, 126, 148
    shapes, 67, 76, 88, 90, 139, 141, 146
Spoon, plastic, 140
Stapler, 31, 40, 144
Starch, liquid, 60, 114, 149
Stencils, 61, 105, 124
Stickers, 12, 28, 31, 78, 83, 86, 103–104, 143, 148, 150
    flower, 32
    foil star, 122
    seasonal, 51, 56, 101, 131, 152
String, 106, 116, 124
Styrofoam, 32
    balls, 34
    scraps, 110
Suction cups, 115
Sun catcher, 80, 98
Switch plate cover, 101

T

Tagboard, 118
Tape, 77, 108, 124–126, 134, 138, 140, 144
    book, 61
    clear, 14–15, 29–30, 86, 88, 98, 106, 130–131, 141, 147
    clear packing, 24, 61
    magnetic, 12–14, 16, 47, 62, 69–70, 73, 85–87, 94
    masking, 74, 88, 90, 142–143
Teacher Appreciation Day, 14–15, 37, 74
Thanksgiving, 39, 59, 113, 118, 121
Toothbrush, 147

Toothpicks, 97, 116–118
Tray
    plastic, 74, 101, 114, 126, 130
    warming, 113
Twine, 38, 82

V
Valentine's Day, 12, 19, 21, 89, 91, 99, 112, 115, 123, 125, 129, 133, 148
Velcro, self-adhesive, 85, 94
Vinyl,
    clear, 61, 105
    shelf liner, 76
Votive holders, 114

W
Wallpaper scraps, 16, 37, 46, 70, 73, 83, 85, 101, 109
Washers, metal, 38, 69
Weaving bands, 58
Wire
    plastic-coated, 150
    seasonal garland, 32, 86
Wrapping paper
    Bubble Blowing Wrapping Paper, 139
    Bubble-Wrap Paper, 138
    foil, 122–123, 140
    Salty Wrapping Paper Sensation, 140
    scraps, 81, 100–101, 104, 109, 129, 134
    tubes, 147
Wrapping Paper Bonanza, 141

Y
Yarn, 16, 21–22, 31, 48, 59, 67, 73, 80, 82, 86, 90, 106, 111, 124–125, 134, 144